Fixtures and CHUCKS for Woodturning

Everything You Need to Know to Secure Wood on Your Lathe

REVISED AND EXPANDED EDITION *by Doc Green*

FOX CHAPEL
PUBLISHING

© 2024 by Clarence R. Green and Fox Chapel Publishing Company, Inc.

Fixtures and Chucks for Woodturning, Revised and Expanded Edition is an original work, first published in 2024 by Fox Chapel Publishing Company, Inc.

ISBN 978-1-4971-0489-1

The Cataloging-in-Publication Data is on file with the Library of Congress.

Managing Editor: Gretchen Bacon
Acquisitions Editor: Kaylee J. Schofield
Editor: Joseph Borden
Designers: Mike Deppen and Matthew Hartsock
Proofreader: Kelly Umenhofer

To learn more about the other great books from Fox Chapel Publishing, or to find a retailer near you, call toll-free 800-457-9112, send mail to 903 Square Street, Mount Joy, PA 17552, or visit us at *www.FoxChapelPublishing.com*.

We are always looking for talented authors. To submit an idea, please send a brief inquiry to acquisitions@foxchapelpublishing.com.

Printed in China
First printing

ABOUT THE AUTHOR

Clarence "Doc" Green, a retired community college professor with a Ph.D. in physics, is a member of the American Association of Woodturners and his local turning club. He is an active participant in two woodturning forums, "World of Woodturners" and "WoodCentral." Green has been a woodworker for more than 30 years, but turning wood only since 2004. In that time, however, he has thoroughly researched the field of woodturning and wood-holding techniques for the lathe. He is the co-author of *The Theory and Servicing of AM, FM, and FM Stereo Receivers* (Prentice-Hall, 1980) and the author of *Technical Physics* (Prentice-Hall, 1984). Visit his website at *www.docgreenwoodturner.com*.

Here I am at my big lathe, where I tested all the ideas for the chucks and fixtures in this book. As you can see, the shop is crowded but organized, with frequently used items close at hand. And I wouldn't dream of doing anything in the shop without a full cup of coffee close at hand, too!

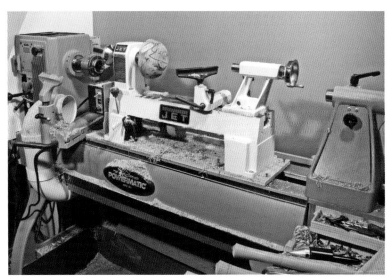

These are my two lathes. Many of the chucks and fixtures for the Powermatic also work on the Jet 10-14 mini lathe.

This is Ol' Rambo, my buddy and loyal companion, who was by my side at every stage of creating this book. He was mindful of his responsibilities and saw to it each and every day that we took a break to go on a big hunt in the woods, to clear the mind and get a bit of exercise as well. (April 1, 1999–August 6, 2013. RIP.)

TABLE OF CONTENTS

INTRODUCTION

If you can't mount a piece of wood on the lathe, you can't turn it.

I learned that soon after I got my first lathe. Even though I had been a woodworker for almost 30 years, turning was completely new to me. I suddenly found myself in a different world. After I learned to use the tools and control the cut, I began to consider making something that amounted to more than a straight stick with a multitude of beads and coves. That's when I realized the importance of knowing how to mount a piece of wood on the lathe.

There is a wealth of information available on tool manipulation and sharpening, and entire books dedicated to making bowls, boxes, goblets, and pens. But information on how to *attach* various pieces on the lathe is not so neatly packaged. It is scattered throughout the other material on an as-needed basis. Some methods are skipped entirely.

The objective of this book is to collect and assemble the information on fixing and chucking methods into one volume. Because many useful chucks and fixtures are not available commercially, you must make them yourself. I'll give you detailed instructions for making fixtures that range in complexity from a simple screw chuck to a complete vacuum chucking system. But don't panic. You do not need to build or buy every single tool and gadget that you see. There's almost always more than one way to perform a certain task. You get to choose the one that you prefer.

A discussion of fixing and chucking methods won't mean much if it is not related to making actual things. That's why I emphasize practical applications for the methods I describe—more than 30 projects that show you how to use the various chucks and fixtures. After all, the objective of turning wood is not to acquire a lathe and a shop full of tools and gadgets. The real objective is to make things out of wood. The variety of objects that can be made in this remarkable medium is astounding.

A part of the challenge of woodturning is designing and building fixtures to mount an unusual piece on the lathe. Most turners eagerly accept this challenge and take pride in their ability to be clever and inventive when faced with a demanding situation.

Among woodturners, it is a compliment if you can produce a piece that prompts the question, "How did you do that?" Often, the real question is, "How did you mount that piece on the lathe?" Artistic and creative genius must be supported by technical knowledge. If you lack technical facility, you may never be able to realize your artistic vision.

And so we come back to what I realized a long time ago: If you can't mount a piece of wood on the lathe, you can't turn it. That's what led me to write this book, which aims to help you with one technical aspect of woodturning.

Let the fun begin.

CHAPTER 1

DRIVE CENTERS AND LIVE CENTERS

Essentials for Spindle Turning

Most turners learn the basics by practicing on a long, skinny stick known as a spindle. It's oriented so that the wood grain runs parallel to the lathe's axis. A roughing gouge, a spindle gouge, and a skew turn the stock from square to round and form a variety of beads and coves. Usually, nothing tangible remains except an odd-shaped stick and a pile of shavings. Such is the nature of the learning process.

Held at the ends. To turn chair legs and other types of spindles, you use sharp centers to grip the wood at either end.

Some experienced turners make spindles almost exclusively, crafting parts for chairs, legs for tables and stools, or balusters for stairs. Others move on to turning bowls, platters, various vessels, and a host of other items ranging from pens to peppermills. However, these turners don't abandon spindle-turning altogether. They frequently turn a finial, a base for a pedestal bowl, or the body of a bottle stopper, all of which are spindles. Even a tall vase is oriented on the lathe like a spindle.

Because spindle turning is fundamental, it is the obvious first topic in learning how to mount wood on the lathe. But spindle turning, or turning between centers, takes many forms. That's why you'll find instructions in this chapter for preparing a blank for a hollow form or a vase, not just for long, skinny pieces.

What Holds a Spindle in Place?

In most cases, a spindle is mounted between centers, held in compression with a drive center in the headstock and a live center at the tailstock, each one jammed into the center of the blank. You can also use a self-centering scroll chuck to grip one end of a spindle, a technique I'll explain later in this chapter.

A drive center has to engage the spindle firmly enough to keep it spinning when you move a turning tool into the wood. At the opposite end, the live center rests in a small hole in the work to keep it on axis and to apply the pressure required to keep the drive center firmly seated.

There are two main types of drive centers: *Spur* centers have two or four chisel-shaped spurs surrounding a central point. A *stebcenter* has a ring of sawtooth-shaped teeth surrounding a spring-loaded central point.

A four-spur drive center works best in the end grain of seasoned wood. A two-spur center works better in the side grain of green

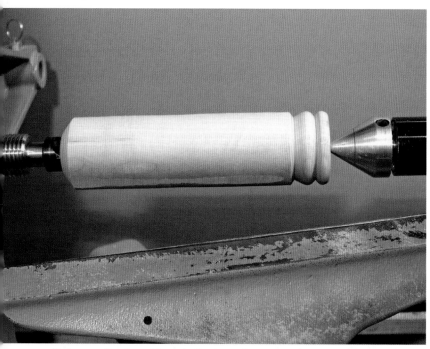

Between Centers. The spindle shown in progress is mounted between centers, held by the drive center at the headstock and the cone center at the tailstock.

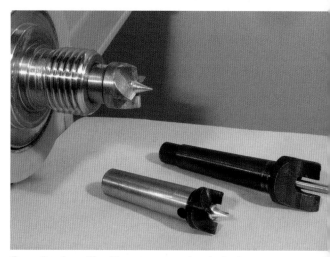

Spur Centers. The Morse taper on the shaft of a drive center locks into the headstock spindle. Also shown are a four-spur and two-spur center.

Stebcenters. Shown here are two types of stebcenters, one meant to fit in a scroll chuck, the other to fit in the headstock spindle. The spring-loaded center pin and the ring of saw teeth give a stebcenter good holding power.

Live Centers. A live center fits in the tailstock ram. Here, a cone center is installed. Two cup centers and a point center are shown underneath.

blanks for bowls; the spurs, aligned with the wood grain, penetrate the wood deeper.

A stebcenter doesn't penetrate the wood as deeply as a spur center does, so it's less likely to split the wood. That's why a stebcenter is preferred for small spindle blanks that are hard and brittle. Many turners favor a stebcenter because it allows them to check the progress of a turning without turning off the lathe or removing the work. Loosening the tailstock slightly allows the stebcenter's spring-loaded center to push the work away from the sawtooth ring, so the work remains centered but stops turning, even though the lathe continues to run.

Live centers take many forms, but two are used most often. A *cup* center has a fairly sharp ring, or cup, surrounding a central point. There's another type of tailstock fixture, also called a cup center, that resembles an inverted cone. It's used to center spindles that can't be held any other way. A *cone* center is, obviously, cone-shaped. Both types spin freely on bearings around the shaft that fits in the tailstock.

Live-Center Accessories. Some live centers are designed to hold multiple heads like those shown here. From left to right: a bull nose cone, a live center adaptor, and a point center.

How to Find the Center of a Spindle

There are several ways to find a spindle's center. The quickest is to simply eyeball it. With practice, you can get pretty good at doing it this way. You can achieve somewhat better accuracy by using a small disk with a hole in its center. Move the disk around until it looks centered, then mark the stock through the center hole. This method works especially well on odd-shaped stock that may have come from the firewood pile.

The classical method is to draw lines between opposite corners of milled stock. This will locate the center precisely on stock that is square or rectangular, or even on a piece whose cross section is a parallelogram. With round stock, a center finder is quite accurate if you use it carefully.

If the stock isn't exactly square or rectangular, draw a 45-degree angle from each corner; the intersecting lines will form a small figure whose center you can easily eyeball.

For very irregular stock, use a compass as a scribe to draw lines parallel to each face: The distance between the compass points should be slightly less than half the smallest distance across the piece. The scribed lines will form a small figure on the piece. Eyeball its center and mark the spot.

Centering Disk. A simple tool to find the center.

Center Finder. An inexpensive tool like this allows you to draw two lines across the piece that intersect at the center. It will also work on stock that is perfectly square.

How to Seat a Drive Center

If you're using a spur center, drill a small hole at the centerpoint on each end to make it easier to locate and seat the centers. (You can skip the holes if you're turning a soft wood like pine or poplar.) It's best to seat a spur center with the work off the lathe. Use a brass hammer or a wooden mallet to tap the center in place. Hitting it with a conventional steel hammer will damage the end of the Morse taper. If you try to pound the work onto the drive center when the center is installed in the headstock spindle, you risk damaging the headstock bearings.

By contrast, you need only a small dimple in the center of the blank to seat it on the centerpoint of a stebcenter. Once you've positioned the spindle between the points of the tailstock live center and the stebcenter, tighten the tailstock. The pressure forces the stebcenter's center point to retract, and its teeth will engage the end of the work.

PROJECT: **TURN AN OVAL TOOL HANDLE**

Many turners who make their own tool handles argue that an oval-shaped handle is better than a round one. An oval handle is easier to grip and it won't roll on a flat surface.

Step one. Mount the blank between centers and turn it round, with the hand grip section next to the tailstock. Loosen the tailstock and shift the blank to move the live center to one side of the original centerpoint. This offset will cause wood to be removed from only one side of the piece, producing half the oval.

Step two. Shift the blank again to move the live center to the other side of the center point. This will produce the other half of the oval. Finally, center the handle again to part it off. Shifting the center very slightly has a rather large effect on the shape of the handle, so proceed carefully. You need to remove only a small amount of wood to produce the oval, so take light cuts, stop the lathe, and check the result.

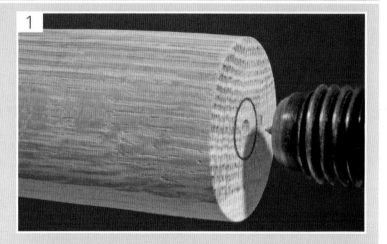

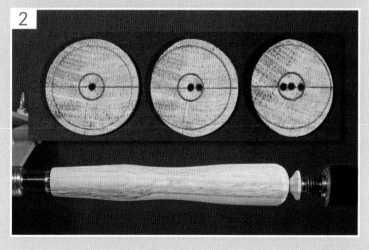

Inset Tenon

Sometimes it is advantageous to form a tenon that actually lies below the surface of the surrounding wood rather than one that extends out from it. This is done by cutting a circular groove into the surface and having the interior wall become the tenon. The chuck jaws reach into the groove to grip the inset tenon.

This technique, for example, saves having to make one waste block when turning a plate from a thin blank. The inset tenon is formed on the side of the blank that will become the top of the plate. It will be removed when the plate is hollowed, after the inset tenon has served its purpose.

The procedure is to first mark the diameter of the desired tenon, and then cut the groove on the outside of that diameter. Make the groove wide enough for the chuck jaws to fit into, and shape the interior wall to match the type of chuck jaws you are using, whether dovetail or straight.

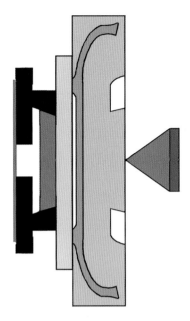

An inset tenon formed by jam chucking a blank against a flat surface.

Flatten an Irregular Blank

Suppose you have a thin blank of nonuniform thickness with rough surfaces on both sides, perhaps from a chain saw. The rough surfaces complicate the use of waste blocks. Further, the blank may be too thin for a faceplate because of the resulting screw holes. What to do?

One solution is to jam the blank against a flat surface (backing plate) and form an inset tenon. At the same time, you can begin to clean up and level the exposed surface. As long as the groove

A rough blank has an uneven surface, making it difficult to use a waste block. In these instances, a flat surface (backing plate) and inset tenon can come in handy.

that forms the tenon is cut cleanly, the surface roughness on the face of the blank will not matter.

The next step is to mount the blank in a scroll chuck using the inset tenon. You can then level and smooth the remaining surface and true up the edge of the blank. A waste block can be applied to the smoothed surface so the blank can be reversed as necessary to complete the piece.

It is not unusual for the faces of such a blank to be uneven so that the blank will not seat solidly against the jam chuck. In this case, small wedges can be used to steady the blank and to adjust its orientation a small amount. If the wedges tend to fly away, as they sometimes do when the lathe is running, a small piece of double-sided tape between the wedge and the backing plate will hold them in place.

A blank jammed against a backing plate.

A blank mounted in the chuck.

A completed inset tenon.

A blank after being turned true.

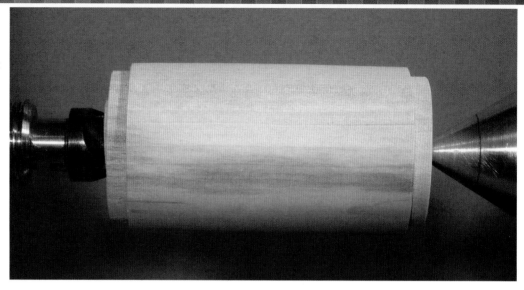

A Trued-up Blank. The blank has been turned to a cylinder and tenons cut on each end.

Truing a Spindle Blank

Turning work between centers is sometimes just the first step. You then hold the work in a scroll chuck to complete the piece. (See Chapter 3 for more on scroll chucks.) That's what many people do to turn drawer knobs, hollow vessels, and a variety of other objects.

To true the blank, mount it between centers, turn it to round, and take it down to the desired diameter. Then, cut tenons on one or both ends that are sized to fit the jaws of the chuck you'll use later. If the chuck has dovetail jaws (see page 37), cut the tenon at an angle to match that of the jaws. Be sure to cut a square shoulder at the end of the tenon so the chuck will seat firmly against the work.

Truing a Blank for a Hollow Form

A vase or hollow form is roughed out between centers, like any other spindle turning. But because the blank is typically quite large, it's a good idea to seat the drive center in a recess, which will hold it much more securely. This is an especially important step if you're working with degraded wood that's too soft to hold a drive center securely.

Recessed Centering. This cutaway view shows a safe way to seat centers in a large or heavy blank. Use a Forstner bit the same diameter as the drive center to drill the recesses.

Spindle-Turned Vessel. This section of spalted walnut log will become a hollow vessel. It's mounted between centers in order to turn its outside profile.

Use a Forstner or spade bit to drill a ½" (13mm)-deep hole the same diameter as the drive center. Seating the drive center in the hole makes it virtually impossible for the blank to move sideways, get out of balance, and come off the lathe. Drill another hole for the center at the tailstock end.

Once you've mounted the blank between centers and trued it up, shape the outside profile. Near the tailstock end, which is the bottom of the vessel, cut a tenon sized to fit the jaws of your scroll chuck. Then flip the work end for end, mount the tenon in the chuck, and hollow the vessel.

Taking Shape. Here, I've formed the outside of the vessel and its base. Below the base, next to the tailstock, is the tenon that will support the vessel in a scroll chuck while the interior is hollowed.

Hollow Forms from Punky Wood

Wood that has decayed to the point at which it has lost most of its strength is termed punky. It may be soft and fibrous or granular so that it crumbles easily. Why deal with such wood, since good wood is easy to find? Punky wood is frequently spalted, containing intricate patterns and colorations that many woodturners favor.

If the wood is significantly degraded, it may require firming up where the centers contact it. Drill the ends of the blank to form recesses for the centers. Apply a few drops of thin cyanoacrylate glue and allow it to wick into the wood, then seat the centers.

If the bottoms of the recesses are ragged and irregular with a lot of tearout, pack fine sawdust into the bottom of the hole before applying the cyanoacrylate glue. Admittedly, this is pushing the limits of working with degraded wood.

If the drive center looks as if it won't stay firmly seated, turn a tenon for a scroll chuck before you do any other shaping. That way, you can switch to the chuck if the drive center tends to break loose and spin inside its recess.

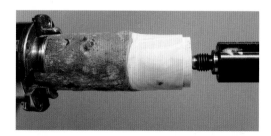

Partially Trued. A spindle blank in the first stage of being trued. It is mounted between a scroll chuck and a live center. At the tailstock end, it has been turned and given a tenon.

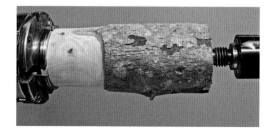

Reversed. Here, the same blank has been reversed, with the tenon held in the scroll chuck. It is ready for more truing-up.

Scroll Chucks and Spindles

Spindle stock that is very nearly square or circular can be held at the headstock end by the jaws of a chuck instead of using a drive center, assuming, of course, that the stock will fit into the chuck jaws. If you hold the blank in a chuck, it does not have to remain in compression to stay securely fixed on the lathe. You can relax the force exerted by the tailstock to very nearly zero. This is a great advantage when turning long slender spindles.

The part of the spindle that fits inside the jaws can't be turned. There is a way to work around that problem.

First, find and mark the center on both ends of the blank. (The marks can be offset from the actual center to balance the grain, center the pith, or offset the blank to avoid sapwood.)

Insert one end into the chuck and close the jaws until they lightly grip the piece. Bring up the tailstock and fit the point of the live center on the center mark on the blank. Advance the live center until it punctures the mark, then alternately tighten the chuck and advance the live center until both ends of the blank are secure.

Turn an inch or so of the blank near the tailstock end to round and form a tenon. You can then do a bit of roughing on the rest of the blank just to clean it up, but don't go too far with this because the blank is not likely to be centered at the headstock end.

Insert the tenon into the chuck and bring the tailstock up to engage the center point on the end opposite the tenon. You can now true up the rest of the blank.

How to Remove a Completed Spindle from the Lathe

In use, the ends of many spindles are hidden. It does not matter whether marks from the drive and live centers remain on the finished spindle. Chair legs and rungs are examples. For other spindles, though, you'll want to remove the lathe marks.

To do that, you must remove the same wood that holds the piece on the lathe. You have to compromise. Turn most of the wood away, but leave a small nubbin to support the piece. Once the piece is off the lathe, you can remove the nubbin.

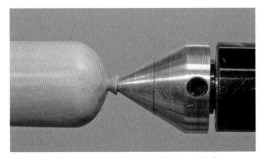

Nubbin. The first step in removing a spindle turning from the lathe is to shape the tailstock end so only a small nubbin remains.

It is best to shape the nubbin like a cone rather than a cylinder. The extra material near the point of the live center makes the nubbin less likely to split apart and cause the piece to come off the lathe prematurely.

You must plan ahead and be sure the blank is somewhat longer than what you need for the finished piece. And you must be prudent in deciding how much of the nubbin can be turned away without getting it so small that it breaks while the lathe is still running.

Friction Drive for Spindle-Turning Practice

A friction drive allows a spindle to stop rotating in the event of a catch or some other unplanned event where the tool digs into the wood.

You can buy a friction drive, but it's easy to make one. A plywood disc ½" (13mm) thick and about 2½" (64mm) in diameter serves as the body of the drive. A tenon allows it to be mounted in a scroll chuck. A nail about ³⁄₁₆" (5mm) in diameter is epoxied into the disc and cut to form the center pin.

When using the friction drive, be sure the headstock end of the practice spindle is cut square so that it makes good contact with the disk of the friction drive.

Advance the tailstock just until the blank is snug. Bring the tool rest into position, start the lathe, and make a cut. If the blank slips too readily, tighten the tailstock some more. If it does not slip under a fairly heavy cut, ease up a little on the tailstock.

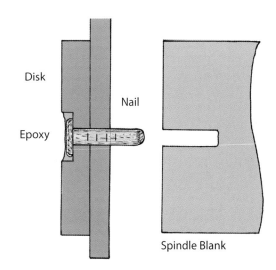

Disk

Nail

Epoxy

Spindle Blank

Friction Drive. This spindle-holder consists of a disk shaped to fit in a scroll chuck and the stub of a nail protruding from its center. The tailstock applies pressure to hold the spindle against the friction drive, and the nail keeps the workpiece centered. If you get a catch with a tool, the drive will let the spindle slip.

PROJECT: TURN A FINIAL OR AN ICICLE FOR AN ORNAMENT

You can make this turning, suitable for a tree ornament or an adornment for a lidded vessel, with the blank mounted in a scroll chuck, as described below. The basic procedure is to turn a tenon at the tailstock end and shape the piece, working from the tailstock end, with the chuck and tailstock keeping it centered.

Some turners prefer to work in the opposite direction, so that the tip of the finial is at the tailstock end. With this approach, the very tip of the finial is formed while the piece is still securely mounted. However, you can't easily do trial fits of the tenon.

Step one. Mount a suitable blank between a scroll chuck and a cone center. The base of the finial will be at the tailstock end.

Step two. At the tailstock end, turn the tenon that will be used to mount the finial. Undercut the base if necessary for a seamless fit. Pull the tailstock back to check the fit as required.

Step three. Shape the top of the base and begin forming the details, working from the tailstock toward the headstock. Sand the features as you go.

Step four. Relax the tailstock pressure and part off the completed finial at the tip. Lightly sand the tip to clean up any torn fibers. A sanding pad held in a Jacobs chuck may be helpful when sanding the tip of the finial.

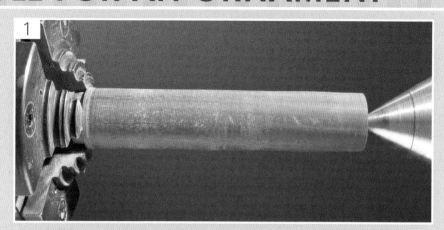

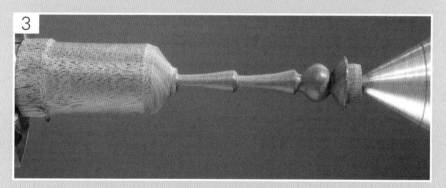

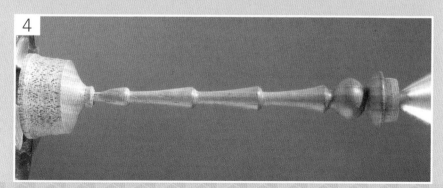

PROJECT: **TURN AN EGG**

This bit of whimsy provides a use for scraps of wood that are too small for other uses and allows you to practice turning a smooth curve. If all goes well, you end up with an egg that can be displayed almost anywhere or placed in a shallow bowl or platter that you've turned. After you've made a few, you will be able to make one in just a few minutes. People love 'em!

This project demonstrates that if one end of the spindle is held by a chuck, and if it is not very long, it may be possible to completely finish the tailstock end while the piece is still on the lathe. In this case, the nubbin is ultimately turned completely away.

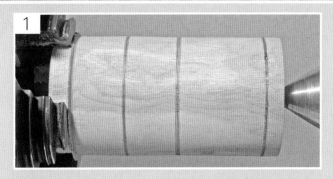

Step one. Mount a suitable blank between a scroll chuck and a cone center. Turn it to a cylinder. Make a line on the cylinder where you want the largest diameter of the egg. Make another line to the right of this one to indicate where the smaller end of the egg will be. Then, to the left of the largest diameter, make a line to designate the other end of the egg. There are no hard-and-fast rules about an egg's shape. Just be sure that one end has a smaller radius than the other.

Step two. Form the shape of the egg. You can reduce the tailstock end down to a small nubbin, but leave enough wood at the headstock end to support the egg in the next step.

Step three. To remove the nubbin at the tailstock end, gradually reduce its diameter as you finish shaping that end. To take the stress off the nubbin, move the tailstock back just before the nubbin drops. The objective is to cut the nubbin free rather than have it twist off or break away.

Step four. Finish as much of the headstock end as you can without risking breaking the egg. Make the final cut. Cup one hand around the egg but don't grip it. With either a small detail gouge or a skew, make a final cut to drop the egg.

The completed egg.

CHAPTER 2

FACEPLATES AND SCREW CHUCKS
Essentials for Bowl Turning and More

A faceplate consists of a flange with a hub that threads onto the headstock spindle. The flange is attached with screws to a flat surface on the blank, and the combination is then mounted on the spindle. A faceplate provides the strongest attachment for large pieces. A blank is nearly always mounted on a faceplate in the side-grain orientation, which is almost synonymous with making bowls and platters.

This chapter explains how to position a faceplate on a blank and what types of screws can be used. I'll provide tips for mounting a faceplate on end-grain wood, along with a few precautions. Also, I'll give instructions for making a faceplate extension, for making a screw chuck, and finally, for making your own faceplate out of wood or medium-density fiberboard (MDF).

The most secure hold. A faceplate screwed in place provides the strongest hold, especially for big, odd-shaped blanks like the one shown here.

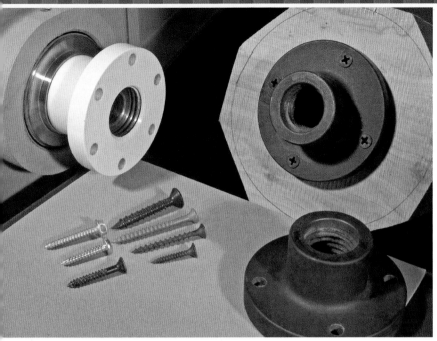

Secure Attachment. A faceplate is the strongest way to hold work on the lathe. The faceplate is screwed to the workpiece and threaded onto the headstock. Depending on the size of the work, you can use drywall screws, sheet metal screws, or even lag screws.

Extra Support. Roughing out even a medium-sized bowl blank like the one shown here produces large impact forces when the projecting corners strike the tool. To counteract that, use larger screws to mount the faceplate and bring the tailstock up for added support.

Faceplates and Bowl Blanks

Roughing out a bowl blank—turning it true and shaping its outside—is one of the more demanding woodturning applications. The centrifugal forces generated when a large, out-of-balance bowl blank spins can put a heavy load on the screws holding the blank on the faceplate. Further, the impact forces produced while turning an out-of-round workpiece only add to the stress the screws must withstand.

Typical faceplate diameters range from 2" to 8" (51 to 203mm). Conventional wisdom says you should use the largest-diameter faceplate that will fit the piece. In fact, it depends upon the wood and your manner of turning. If you take light cuts, you can use a small faceplate if it is mounted on sound wood. But if you turn spalted, degraded wood or take heavy cuts, use a larger faceplate. Either way, use the tailstock for additional support whenever possible, especially when turning a large blank.

PROJECT: **MAKE YOUR OWN FACEPLATE**

If you have a spindle tap, you can make a faceplate using either MDF or a good grade of plywood. While such a faceplate may not be as strong as one made of metal, it is still functional. The procedure for making it is basically the same as that for making a vacuum chuck with a threaded hub described in Chapter 9 (page 122).

MDF and plywood have a tendency to delaminate along planes parallel to the surface when stress is applied to an area that is small in cross section. The design of the faceplate compensates for this by making the hub disk larger in diameter, using screws as reinforcements, and coating the perimeter of the hub disk with epoxy.

The faceplate I made using ¾" (19mm) thick MDF is 6" (152mm) in diameter. You can adjust the dimensions as you see fit. To test this faceplate, I mounted it on a 12" (305mm) sycamore bowl blank (see photo) and then roughed it out, using tailstock support and taking fairly heavy cuts. It passed the test; the threads were undamaged, and the faceplate did not jam onto the headstock spindle.

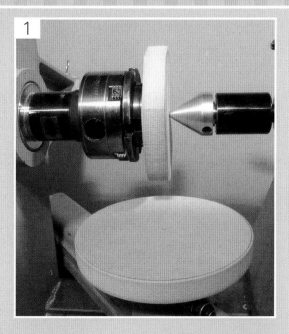

This is the test I did for the faceplate I made.

Step one. Cut out and true up a face disk and a smaller hub disk. Leave the face disk slightly larger than its final diameter, but turn the hub disk to size. I used a diameter of 4½" (114mm) for the hub disk on my 6" (152mm) faceplate.

Step two. Jam the hub disk against the jaws of a scroll chuck and shape a tenon with a diameter as large as the jaws of your scroll chuck will hold. I used 2¾" (70mm). Make the tenon ¼" (6mm) deep. Remove the disk from the lathe and draw a circle on it 3½" (89mm) in diameter. Drill and countersink six holes equally spaced around the circle for the reinforcing screws. I used #6 coarse-thread drywall screws 1" (25mm) long.

MAKE YOUR
PROJECT: **OWN FACEPLATE** *CONTINUED*

Step three. Draw a circle on the face disk equal to the diameter of the hub disk. Apply a thin coat of epoxy to the hub disk and place it within the circle. Clamp it between the live center of the tailstock and the jaws of the chuck. Install the six reinforcing screws. After the epoxy cures, start the lathe and true the edge of the face disk to correct any inaccuracies in positioning the hub disk.

Step four. Drill and countersink holes near the perimeter of the face disk for attaching it to the workpiece. I drilled holes ¼" (6mm) in diameter for six screws and positioned the holes about ½" (13mm) from the edge of the disk.

Step five. In anticipation of cutting the threads, mount the faceplate in a scroll chuck, using the tenon on the hub disk. Follow the procedure given in Chapter 9 (page 122) and cut the threads. Then remove the faceplate from the chuck, remove the chuck, and thread the faceplate on the headstock spindle, using a spacer ring as required.

Step six. Reduce the thickness of the hub disk so that the end of the headstock spindle nearly reaches the surface of the faceplate. Don't overdo it, because the end of the spindle must not extend past the surface of the faceplate when it is in use. Be sure the back of the hub disk seats flat against the bearing surface behind the threads on the headstock spindle. Apply a layer of epoxy to the perimeter of the hub disk and then coat the entire surface, including the threads, with several coats of lacquer sanding sealer. The photo at left shows the completed faceplate.

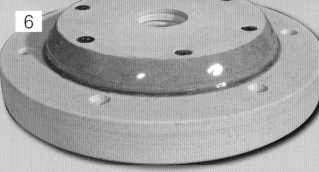

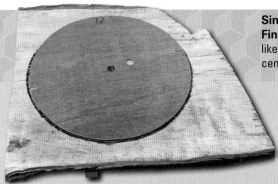

Simple Center-Finder. Use a disk like this to eyeball the center of a bowl blank.

Centering the Faceplate

A collection of different-sized disks with holes in their centers makes a great time saver when centering a faceplate on a bowl blank. Pick the largest disk that fits within the edges of the bowl blank and mark the center. You can then center the faceplate on the mark by eye, looking down through the hole in the hub, or draw a circle centered on the mark that the faceplate will fit inside.

You can buy a faceplate center marker that can be used to center a faceplate on a mark or to mark the center of a faceplate that's already installed. It consists of a rod, drilled down the center, that fits inside the threaded hub of a faceplate. A pointer fits in the center hole.

To center a faceplate on a mark, extend the pointer and place it on the mark. Then let the pointer guide the faceplate into position. To mark the center of a faceplate that's already mounted, simply drop the rod into the faceplate hub and tap the pointer.

You can easily make a center-marker from a piece of spindle stock and a long nail. To make the fixture with the nail, mount a blank about 3" (76mm) long between a scroll chuck and a cone center. True up the blank and use a Jacobs chuck to drill the hole for the nail. (I picked a nail used to install gutters, cutting it to length.) Drill a hole that's very slightly larger than the nail so it will fit snugly but still slide easily. Turn the shaft so it matches the threaded hole in the faceplate. Finally, shape the top end and part it off.

The center marker will also work with a scroll chuck holding the foot of a bowl whose center is unmarked, because the faceplate and the scroll chuck will have the same thread diameter. Remove the chuck from the headstock spindle, with the bowl still mounted in the chuck. Then insert the center marker into the threaded part of the chuck, tap the nail, and it will be done. Additionally, if you have an unmounted bowl with an unmarked center, you can temporarily attach a chuck to the tenon and then use the marker to locate the center.

To make a simpler item for positioning only, turn a blank to fit the threaded hole in the faceplate and bring it to a point at the tailstock end. Shape the top. This device can only position and hold a faceplate on a center mark because the wooden point isn't strong enough to create a center mark on the work.

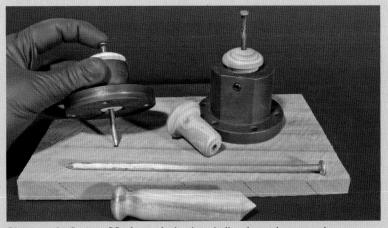

Shopmade Center-Markers. A simple spindle, shown between the two faceplates, lets you position a faceplate on a center point. Upper left, the faceplate is being centered on the mark. Upper right, tapping the nail will mark the position of the faceplate. In the center is a body for the fixture. To the front is a gutter nail and a simpler fixture for centering a faceplate.

Mounting the Faceplate

The screws you use to attach a faceplate should be in proportion to the size of the workpiece. If you work with blanks that weigh only a pound or two (0.45 to 0.9 kg), you can use small screws. But if you work with blanks that may weigh more than 50 lb. (22.6 kg), then use lag screws and a substantial faceplate.

There's a lot of energy in a spinning blank. For example, the rim of a 16" (406mm) blank running at 600 rpm is traveling about 28 mph (45km/h). The energy it contains is equivalent to having it fall from a height of 14' (4.3m). If that blank comes off the lathe, it can cause serious injury.

Many turners warn against using drywall screws because they are brittle. However, I often use them to mount small pieces. I typically use coarse-thread #6 drywall screws, 1¼" (32mm) long, for mounting faceplates on bowl blanks up to about 8" (203mm) in diameter. For smaller pieces of sound wood, say 5" (127mm) in diameter, I normally use 1" (25mm)-long #6 screws. For workpieces in the 10" to 12" (254 to 305mm) range, 1¼" or 1½" (32 or 38mm)-long #10 sheet metal screws are excellent because they are less brittle. For even larger work, use #12 or larger sheet-metal screws or lag screws.

If the wood is dry and hard, you may have to drill pilot holes for the screws. You can tell if they are needed when you begin to install a screw. If the screw gets tight quickly and your power driver tends to labor, back up and drill the holes. The time it takes to drill pilot holes is negligible compared to the time it takes to remove a broken screw or one with a stripped-out head.

Always be on the alert for any vibration or looseness that may result from broken or loose screws. This is especially important when turning a large, out-of-round piece. Stop the lathe periodically and give the piece a good, stout, two-handed wiggle. Any movement at all indicates that there is a problem that must be addressed. Also, do this immediately after getting a significant catch or having any other mishap that delivers a sharp blow to the piece.

Mounting a Faceplate on End Grain

Screws do not hold well in end-grain wood. The threads cut the wood fibers adjacent to the body of the screw so it's relatively easy for the screw to pull out. Nevertheless, you can screw a faceplate to end grain successfully if you keep these three points in mind.

Always drill a properly-sized pilot hole. The pilot hole's diameter should be approximately equal to the root diameter of the screw thread. The pilot hole significantly reduces the amount the wood is compressed and damaged around the screw.

Mounted on End Grain. An end-grain bowl blank mounted on a faceplate. Tailstock support is used whenever possible.

Use longer screws. For example, if a screw 1¼" (32mm) long would be appropriate for face grain, use a 1⅝" (41mm) screw for end grain. Use the largest-diameter screws that are practical. Avoid fine-thread screws for end-grain wood.

Don't overtighten the screws. You can use a powered driver to run the screw most of the way in, but use a screwdriver to do the final seating by hand. Stop when the screw seats. Don't give it a final push to lock it down. That can break the wood fibers between the threads and allow the screw to pull out with remarkable ease.

Faceplate Screws and Punky Wood

If you have to mount a faceplate on a blank that is significantly degraded, the wood may be barely able to hold the screws. Here are three things you can do to improve matters: First, use the largest faceplate you have that will fit the piece. Make an extension (see page 32) if you need to.

Two, use screws somewhat larger in length and diameter than what you would normally use with sound wood.

Three, mount the faceplate but don't tighten the screws. Unscrew the faceplate and apply thin cyanoacrylate glue to the screw holes; it will wick into the holes and firm up the wood. Let the glue cure for a minute or so, then reinstall the faceplate and tighten the screws.

JUMBO
PROJECT: SCREW CHUCK

A screw chuck with a large-diameter bearing surface is more effective in transmitting torque to the workpiece without putting undue stress on the screw. Put differently, you can mount a larger workpiece on one with a larger diameter. It's not just the size of the screw that matters.

Many scroll chucks are supplied with a screw that can be mounted in the chuck jaws to enable it to be used as a screw chuck. However, the chuck jaws themselves act as the bearing surface, which is typically 4" (100mm) or less in diameter. Further, the faces of the jaws are usually smooth and shiny, which is not ideal.

A significant improvement can be made by mounting the screw at the center of a larger plywood disk, which, in turn, is held by the jaws of the scroll chuck. Here is how to do it.

Step one. Begin with two rough-cut disks of ¾" (19mm) plywood of diameters about 7 ½" (190mm) and 4" (100mm). Center the smaller disk on the larger one and attach with glue and screws. This will become the body of the screw chuck.

Step two. Jam the blank against a flat surface. True up and form a tenon on the smaller disk. Make the diameter of the tenon match your chuck jaws when they are almost fully open.

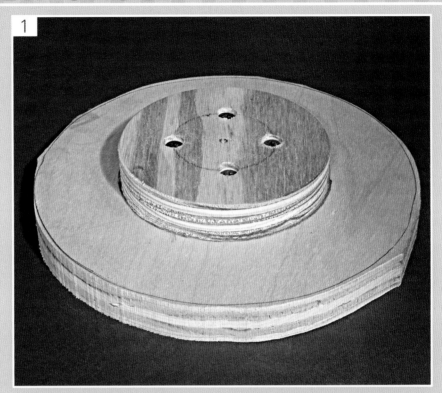

Step three. Mount the blank in your scroll chuck and true up the outer diameter of the larger disk. Drill a hole at the center all the way through the blank. Size the hole so the screw will thread into it with relative ease.

Step four. Drill a clearance hole for the body of the screw. Use a drill press and a 1" (25mm) Forstner bit and center the clearance hole over the hole drilled in Step Three. The depth of this hole determines how much the screw thread will extend beyond face of the disk, which should be about ⅞" (22mm). Proceed carefully. Alternatively, you can mount the blank in a set of Cole jaws to drill the hole, as shown in the photo.

Step five. Thread the screw into the disk assembly. Be sure it is fully seated. Fill the area around the body of the screw with epoxy. Your screw chuck is now complete.

Screw Chucks

It is sometimes preferable to use a center-screw faceplate, also known as a screw chuck, instead of a conventional faceplate. It lets you rough out a small-diameter turning without having to work around the screws of an ordinary faceplate. If the piece must be removed and then rechucked, a screw chuck allows that to be done more quickly and with a better chance of having the rechucked piece run true.

To use a screw chuck, drill a pilot hole into a flat surface of the workpiece; screw it onto the chuck until it seats against the backplate. Don't use a screw chuck in wood that's not sound, or in end grain. The threads may not hold.

You can buy a dedicated screw chuck or use the accessory screw that comes with most scroll chucks. Or you can make your own, attaching it to a conventional faceplate. A shopmade screw chuck can be whatever size you wish to make it. The sidebar on the facing page shows what to do.

Jacobs Chuck. A Jacobs chuck makes a very useful lathe accessory. It fits in either the headstock or tailstock Morse taper and converts the lathe to a horizontal drill press. The Jacobs chuck ensures that any pilot holes you drill—when making a screw chuck, for example—are centered on the stock and square to the face of the work.

Making a Faceplate Extension

I once had a 13" (330mm) bowl blank of spalted beech that had fallen victim to ants. Although the wood was workable, it had a collection of voids exactly where the faceplate needed to go. There was little wood to hold the screws of my 3" (76mm) faceplate, and I didn't have a larger one. So I solved the problem by attaching a larger plywood disk, an extension, to one of my small faceplates.

To make a faceplate extension, follow the procedure for making the center-screw faceplate on page 33, using ¾" (19mm) plywood or MDF. But instead of putting a screw at the center, drill and countersink a ring of equally spaced holes near the circumference of the disk.

In addition to serving as a large faceplate, the extension can serve as a backing plate for jam-chucking, a technique explained in Chapter 5.

Screw Chuck. Most scroll chucks come with a screw accessory. It's gripped in the center of the jaws. The screw threads into a pilot hole drilled in the workpiece and holds it securely.

PROJECT: **A SHOPMADE SCREW CHUCK**

The steps shown here are for a chuck that's 5½" (140mm) in diameter, attached to a 3" (76mm) faceplate. But you can make the chuck any size you like. I used a lag screw ¼" (6mm) in diameter and 1" (25mm) long, but you can substitute another size or type as long as it has a deep thread and a coarse pitch. It all depends on the size of the blanks you want to turn.

Step one. Rough-turn a ¾"-thick (19mm) plywood or medium-density fiberboard (MDF) disk to a diameter slightly greater than its final diameter.

Step two. Remove the disk from the lathe and draw a circle at its center equal to the diameter of the faceplate. Drill a hole at the center somewhat larger than the head of the screw you plan to use. If necessary, make the hole deeper than the thickness of the screw head so that the screw extends farther from the face side of the disk.

Step three. Position the faceplate in the circle and screw it to the disk. Mount the assembly on the lathe. Use a Jacobs chuck in the tailstock to drill a pilot hole for the center screw. True up the outside diameter of the disk and sand the edges smooth.

Step four. Remove the assembly from the lathe and, working through the hole in the faceplate hub, drive the center screw tightly into the pilot hole. Cover the screw head with epoxy.

CHAPTER 3

SCROLL CHUCKS
Handy for Bowl Turning and Spindles

After you acquire a lathe, basic cutting tools, and a means for sharpening them, buy a scroll chuck, even though one is not cheap. The convenience and utility a scroll chuck brings make it well worth the price.

In this chapter, besides giving you the basic techniques for using a scroll chuck to hold bowls, hollow forms, and spindles, I'll show you how to make a reference plate to help re-center a bowl that has been removed from the chuck. I'll also show you how to turn a Morse taper, which holds the reference plate on the tailstock ram.

You will also find instructions for turning a goblet with a lid. Not only will this project give you practice in hollowing, turning decorative features on a small spindle, and fitting one part to another, it also makes a great little gift.

A very versatile chuck. The adjustable, self-centering jaws of a scroll chuck make it a workhorse for holding bowl blanks, spindles, and more.

Anatomy of a Scroll Chuck

As the photo below shows, the body of a scroll chuck contains a flat ring with a spiral groove on one side. This is the scroll. It is free to rotate about the rotational axis of the chuck. The mounts for the jaws, known as sliders, have teeth that engage the scroll and move in or out as the scroll spins.

Scroll Chuck Parts. The large ring in the center is the scroll; its spiral groove makes the chuck self-centering. In front of the scroll are three of the sliders, which engage the scroll and hold the chuck jaws. One of the sliders is in the chuck body in the background. At right are the jaws, which screw onto the sliders. The small ring in the foreground holds the scroll in place. The insert at far left adapts the body to the lathe spindle.

Spindle Adaptor. This accessory screws onto the headstock spindle to provide a different thread size. In this case, it allows chucks with a 1" x 8 tpi thread to be used on a lathe with a 1¼" x 8 tpi spindle. An adaptor eliminates the need to buy multiple chucks if you have more than one lathe.

The sliders' teeth are made so that all the sliders are always equidistant from the center of the chuck. This feature makes a scroll chuck self-centering.

Typical chucks use a threaded insert to attach the chuck to the headstock spindle. If you have two lathes with different spindle sizes, you need to install a spindle adaptor on one lathe so that you can use the chuck on both machines.

Most manufacturers make at least three sizes of scroll-chuck jaws, usually designated as #1, #2, or #3, with #1 jaws being the smallest. Also, many special-purpose jaw sets are available. Changing the jaws from one set to another is a simple five-minute operation. (Jaws aren't interchangeable among brands of chucks.)

The chuck jaws hold the work in one of two ways. They may be closed around a tenon on the foot of a bowl or around a small spindle, which puts the wood in compression. Or, they may be expanded to press against the walls of a recess turned in the workpiece, which puts the wood in tension. The tenon or recess must be turned to match the profile of the jaws. In profile, the jaws are either serrated or dovetail. A tenon for serrated jaws should be straight, while the tenon for dovetail jaws must be tapered to match the shape of the jaws.

With any scroll chuck, you must turn a surface on the workpiece for the ends of the jaws to butt against. This takes the form of a square shoulder at the end of a tenon or a flat surface at the bottom of a recess. Butting the jaws against these surfaces makes it

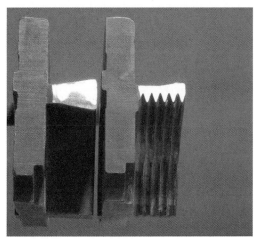

Jaw Profiles. Left, a dovetail jaw. Right, a serrated jaw; it has straight sides, with ridges that bite into a tenon. A tenon or recess in the workpiece must be shaped to match the shape of the jaws, or the chuck won't grip securely.

more likely that the workpiece will run true and adds significantly to the holding power of the jaws.

If, after considerable use, the jaws of a chuck become stiff and hard to adjust, chances are that dust has accumulated around the sliders and in the scroll. Blowing out the dust with compressed air will usually solve the problem.

A Secure Grip. A scroll chuck's jaws must butt against the shoulder of a tenon and the tenon must not contact the bottom of the jaws. Otherwise, the piece will have no natural tendency to center itself and run true. (Two jaws have been removed for the photograph.)

Choosing a Tenon Diameter

A given set of jaws will accept a considerable range of tenon diameters, so you have to decide what diameter to use on a particular piece. A larger-diameter tenon provides more holding power than a small one, but other considerations come into play.

Convenience. A large tenon limits how closely you can work toward the foot of a vessel and adds to the amount of work if you want to remove the tenon rather than incorporate it into the foot of the vessel.

Appearance. Dovetail jaws have only one diameter at which they grip a tenon uniformly, leaving the fewest dents or marks in the work. However, serrated jaws will probably mar the work at any diameter.

Safety. Many turners prefer not to have the chuck jaws opened so far that the sliders extend beyond the body of the chuck, for safety reasons. It is a good idea to file or sand the burrs and sharp corners off the leading edges of the chuck jaws and sliders where they extend beyond the body of the chuck. Your hand *will* contact these at some point, so removing the sharp edges reduces the risk of serious injury.

Knuckle-Banger. When you open a chuck wide, the jaws and sliders protrude past the body and can hit the knuckles of the unwary. The highlighted area shows the sharp corners that should be filed down for safety's sake.

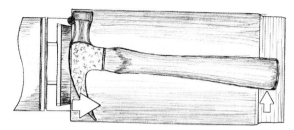

Leverage. The upward force of a turning tool tends to lever the tenon out of the bottom jaw. The farther the cutting tool is from the jaws, the greater the leverage. The effect is the same as pulling a nail with a long-handled hammer instead of a short-handled one.

Leverage. When a tool engages the wood, the rotating wood forces the tool downward against the tool rest, and the tool exerts an upward force on the wood. It's an action and a reaction.

Because the jaws grip the piece a distance away from where the tool contacts the wood, a leverage issue comes into play. It multiplies the force tending to pull the piece from the chuck. Working away from the jaws, as in hollowing the cup of a tall goblet, increases the effect. To minimize the risk of having the work levered out of the chuck, use the largest diameter tenon that's practical.

Torque. For a given vessel, it is less likely the jaws will break loose and spin on the tenon if the tenon is large. For example, if you double the diameter of the tenon, the required sideways force that must be applied to the wood by the jaws is cut in half.

Expanding the Jaws into a Recess

When you want to use a scroll chuck to grip the workpiece in a recess, keep these points in mind:

Wood is not as strong under tension as it is under compression, so be sure you have adequate wood surrounding the recess to withstand the tendency of the expanding jaws to pry it apart. My rule of thumb is to have at least ¾" (19mm) of sound wood surrounding the recess; other turners may want more.

The diameter of the recess relative to the diameter of the blank is also important. If the recess is too small, the chuck jaws may spin inside the recess, and this may cause the blank to come off the lathe. The diameter of the recess should be at least 20 percent of the diameter of the blank, assuming sound wood and a recess that's a bit deeper than the minimum. That is, a 10" (254mm) blank should have a recess at least 2" (51mm) in diameter.

The required depth of the recess depends greatly on the quality of the wood; it must be deeper in wood that is degraded. The shape of the jaws also matters. You can use a relatively shallow recess if the jaws have sharp, crisp edges, as is typical for dovetail jaws. So, with

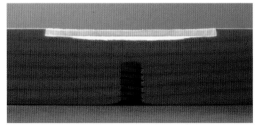

Recess for a Chuck. A cutaway view of a platter, showing the hole for a screw center and the recess in the foot to accommodate a scroll chuck. Although only ⅛" (3mm) deep, the recess has sufficient surface for the chuck jaws to expand against.

dovetail jaws in solid wood, you can use a recess as shallow as ⅛" (3mm) as long as you don't take aggressive cuts.

You also have to consider the effects of leverage when planning the depth of the recess. A deep bowl requires a deeper recess than a shallow bowl or platter.

PROJECT: **MAKE A SPIN TOP**

You do not always have to form a tenon on a workpiece in order to mount it in a scroll chuck. This top, made from a cedar limb, is a case in point. As you make it, complete all the cuts and sanding on the body before turning the handle to its final diameter.

Step one. Mount a short section of limb in a scroll chuck. Use the tailstock to support the work for the initial roughing.

Step two. Round the spindle, then shape and sand the body of the top.

Step three. Bring the handle down its final diameter and shape. Finish by parting off the piece at the top of the handle.

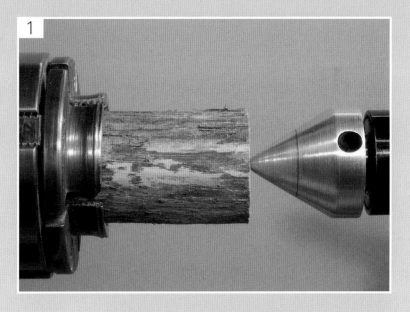

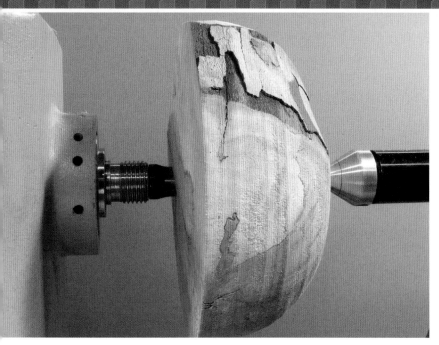

Roughing Between Centers. Mounting a bowl blank between centers lets you make adjustments to orient the grain optimally or eliminate flaws. On this sycamore blank, for example, I shifted the tail center slightly, changing the plane of the face.

Chuck and Drive. When working with large, green bowl blanks, use a two-prong drive center. The one shown here is 2" (51mm) in diameter, designed to fit in a scroll chuck.

Two Ways to Prepare a Bowl Blank for Chucking

Before you can hold a bowl blank with a scroll chuck, you have to shape the outside and turn a tenon or recess for the chuck jaws. This means one of these other methods must be used to hold the blank before it is mounted in the chuck.

Faceplate. As explained in Chapter 2, a faceplate mounts quickly and holds the wood securely. But using a faceplate is not without its drawbacks, chiefly this: Once the faceplate is screwed in place, the blank's orientation is fixed. You can't fine-tune the placement to balance the grain.

Between centers. You can avoid this limitation by mounting the blank between centers. Typically, the drive center is installed on the flat face of the blank, while the live center supports the curved surface. (You often have to chisel or saw away some of the bark on that face to create a palm-sized area that is relatively flat and free of bark so the live center can press securely against solid wood.) To mount a large, green blank, use a two-spur drive center, with the spurs aligned with the wood grain.

Mount the blank with just enough force applied to the tail center to hold it temporarily. Rotate the blank slowly by hand while studying the area close to the rim of the finished bowl. Look for distinguishing features such as sapwood, knots, or voids, and note the pattern of the grain on the cross-grain ends of the blank. Shift the blank as needed to either eliminate faults or make the most of distinctive features. Once you're satisfied, tighten the tailstock center.

After turning the outside of the blank, remove the blank from the lathe and remount it in a scroll chuck. Use the tailstock to apply pressure to the blank to help ensure that the chuck jaws seat firmly and uniformly.

If you did the initial turning with a faceplate, leave it attached until you've finished rechucking the work. Use a cone center to engage the hub of the faceplate. If you turned the blank between centers, let the cone center contact the dimple made by the drive center.

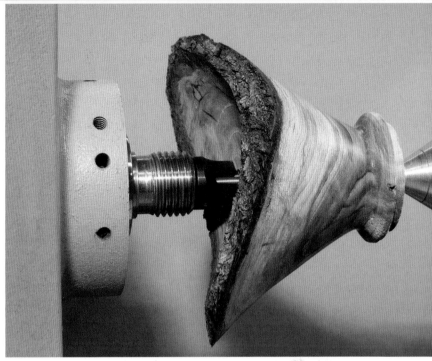

Balance. Natural-edge bowls are turned between centers, so the blank can be shifted as needed to balance the edge on opposite sides of the bowl.

Reversing a Bowl. When you've roughed the outside of a bowl, leave the faceplate on the blank and press the tailstock into the faceplate spindle. That forces the blank against the chuck jaws, ensuring that the blank will be centered and firmly seated when you tighten the chuck. Stabilizing the work in this way allows you to take aggressive cuts at the rim. Of course, you'll have to remove the faceplate to complete the turning.

PROJECT: TURN A GOBLET WITH A LID

A goblet makes a good practice piece because it requires a variety of cuts, and variations in design are virtually unlimited. Admittedly, a wooden goblet isn't very useful. With a lid, though, it becomes a box on a pedestal to hold rings, earrings, and other small trinkets. Making the wall of the goblet fairly thin and uniform isn't as easy as it may seem.

Step one. Mount a 4¼" (108mm)-long hardwood spindle blank between the chuck and tailstock and turn it to 1¼" (32mm) in diameter. Mark the section of the spindle near the tailstock where the taper is to be formed. Make it at least 2½" (64mm).

Step two. Shape the outside profile of the cup. Leave enough wood at the top of the stem to support the work when you hollow the cup.

Step three. Remove the tailstock and hollow the inside of the cup.

Step four. Shape the bottom of the cup, the stem, and the top of the base. Refine the edge of the base and establish its thickness.

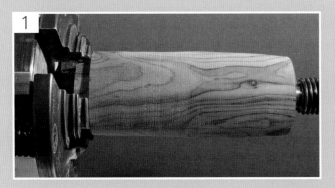

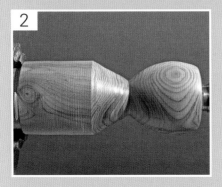

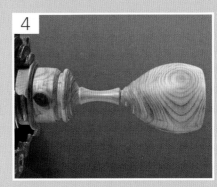

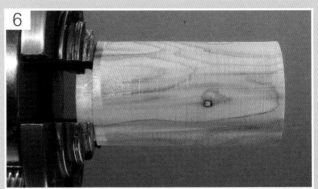

Step five. Part off the goblet, undercutting the base a small amount. Finish the bottom of the base off the lathe.

Step six. Mount a blank for the lid in a scroll chuck, oriented so the top of the lid is next to the chuck jaws.

Step seven. Shape the outside of the lid and turn a flange on its base that will eventually fit inside the rim of the goblet. Do not turn the flange to its final diameter at this point.

Step eight. Hollow the underside of the lid, and then turn the lid flange to its final diameter. Test the fit often as you reduce the diameter.

Step nine. Shape a decorative finial, sanding the details as you go.

Step ten. Complete the top and part it off. In the final stages of turning the finial, stablize the base with the tailstock. Fold a swatch of paper towel and press it into the base to protect the wood from the point of the live center.

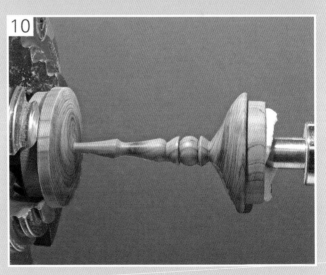

Rechucking a Piece in the Same Position

If you remove a piece from the chuck before you've completed the turning, it won't automatically run true when you put it back in the chuck. But the following techniques can help you minimize the runout, or wobble, and maybe even eliminate it.

Before removing the piece, mark the position of the first jaw. That way, when you rechuck the piece, you can get the jaws exactly where they were before.

If the center of the piece is clearly defined at the tailstock end, use a tailstock center to help align the piece during rechucking. Vases or hollow forms with small openings can be re-centered by pressing a cone center or a bullnose cone into the opening.

Bullnose Cone. This cutaway shows a flat plate fitted over the large end of the cone. The plate can be pressed against the rim of a bowl to align it in the chuck jaws.

If the rim of a bowl is flat, you can use a bullnose cone and a flat disk to square the bowl in the chuck. If you don't have a bullnose cone, consider making a reference plate, described on page 46.

If all else fails, fall back on trial and error, tapping the piece to bring it true before tightening the jaws completely.

Nicely Aligned. Here, I've retracted the reference plate slightly after using it to mount the bowl blank. The uniform space between the bowl rim and the reference plate tells me that the bowl is seated properly and will run true.

Using a Scroll Chuck as a Jam Chuck

You can use a scroll chuck like a jam chuck when reverse-chucking a semi-closed vessel or a bowl with an inward-sloping rim. (Reverse-chucking refers to turning the nearly complete bowl end for end to clean up the base.) In this case, you expand the jaws to provide a seat for the rim. Use blue painter's tape to pad the jaws so they don't scratch or dent the rim. Don't tighten the jaws too much or you may pry the rim apart.

To apply the tape, open the jaws just slightly wider than what's needed to hold the piece. Apply the tape. Close the jaws enough for the rim of the vessel to slip over them,

then tighten the jaws. This keeps the tape from having to stretch as you expand the jaws and makes it easier to feel the force being applied to the rim.

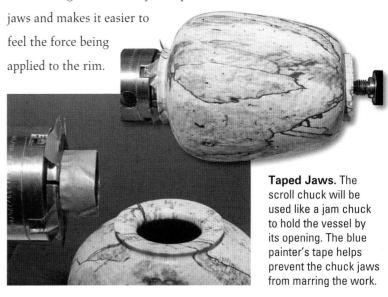

Taped Jaws. The scroll chuck will be used like a jam chuck to hold the vessel by its opening. The blue painter's tape helps prevent the chuck jaws from marring the work.

A Fast Way to True a Small Disk

A scroll chuck can help you quickly transform a roughly-sawn blank of flat stock into a disk. Sandwich the wood between the chuck jaws and the live center. This creates a surprisingly strong hold. The tailstock also leaves a center mark in the disk for future reference.

If you want to make a disk from a fairly thin board, use a cup center instead of a cone center at the tailstock; its centerpoint is less likely to penetrate deeply and split the wood.

To true a disk whose diameter is greater than about three times the diameter of the chuck jaws, use a backing plate (see page 56) instead of the chuck jaws. The plate provides a much larger bearing surface and better frictional contact with the disk.

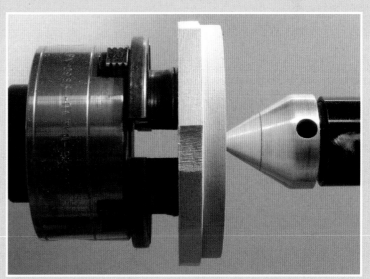

Chuck as Backstop. You can true up a disk by using the tailstock to jam it against the front surface of the chuck jaws. Friction will hold the work in place as you turn it. Here, half the disk has been trued.

MAKE A
PROJECT: REFERENCE PLATE

A disk attached to a Morse-taper spindle and fitted in the tailstock makes a useful fixture for squaring an object in the jaws of a scroll chuck. For lack of a better name, I'll call this disk a reference plate. Here's how to make it:

This project has two parts. First, turn a Morse taper adaptor, which allows the plate to be held in the tailstock ram. Then make the plate itself. These instructions are for a #2 Morse taper, which is 2½" (64mm) long, with the largest diameter of 0.7" (18mm) and the smallest diameter of 0.57" (15mm).

Step one. Mount a 4¼" (108mm) long hardwood spindle blank between the chuck and tailstock and turn it to 1¼" (32mm) in diameter. Mark the section of the spindle near the tailstock where the taper is to be formed. Make it at least 2½" (64mm) long. Turn the spindle to a uniform ¾" (19mm) diameter in this section.

Step two. Use a parting tool and a dial caliper to establish a diameter of 0.6" (15mm) at the tailstock end. Measure 2½" (64mm) from that cut and establish a diameter of 0.72" (18mm).

Step three. Turn away the wood between the cuts to form as uniform a taper as you can manage. Before moving on, be sure you have a way to eject the blank from the tailstock ram in case it gets stuck.

Step four. Refine the fit of the taper. Remove the live center from the tailstock and move the ram up over

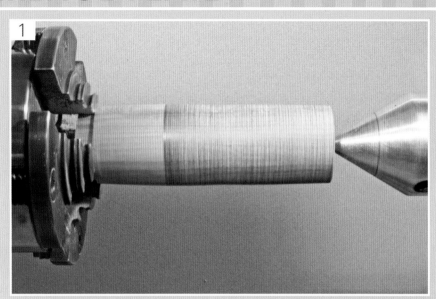

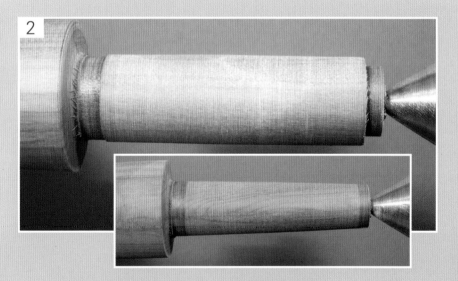

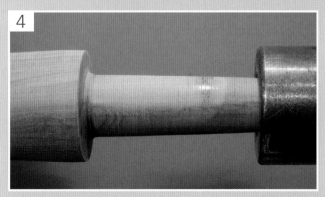

the taper, just short of making contact. Start the lathe and then advance the ram until it makes a very light contact with the taper. It will mark or burnish the wood where it hits the high spots.

Step five. Reinstall the live center and use it to support the end of the blank. Use very fine cuts to knock down the high spots. Continue to check the fit and knock down high spots until nearly all the taper fits into the tailstock. As you get near the final fit, use 100-grit sandpaper instead of a turning tool.

Step six. Cut a disk from a good grade of ½" (13mm) or ¾" (19mm) plywood. Prepare a waste block about 2¼" (57mm) in diameter and ¾" (19mm) thick, with a tenon and a shoulder for the chuck jaws. Glue it to the center of the plywood disk.

Step seven. Mount the disk in the chuck and true its outside edge. Use a Forstner bit to bore a 1" (25mm) hole through the center for the adaptor. Remove the disk from the chuck.

Step eight. Insert the newly formed Morse taper into the headstock spindle. Use the tailstock to keep it seated securely. Mark a line on the adaptor to designate the length of the shoulder that is to appear at the end of the Morse taper. Then reduce the diameter to the right of this line so that it will fit tightly into the hole bored at the center of the disk.

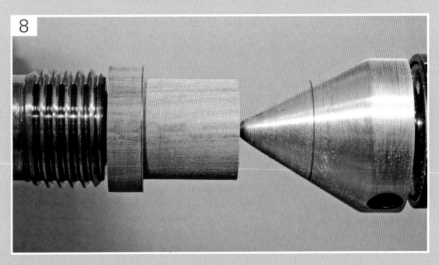

Step nine. Once the disk fits onto the adaptor, press it on with the waste block on the tailstock side. Be sure the disk makes contact with the shoulder. Trim the waste block until it is flush with the end of the adaptor.

Step ten. Remove the disk from the adaptor. If the fit was unusually tight, you can now loosen the fit so that assembly will be easier when the glue is applied. Install the adaptor in the tailstock ram. Screw a chuck onto the headstock and open the jaws to their maximum diameter.

Step eleven. Apply medium cyanoacrylate glue to the hole in the plate; then, very quickly slide the plate over the end of the adaptor, waste block first. Bring the tailstock up to press the disk against the jaws of the chuck. This will square the disk to the axis of the lathe.

Step twelve. After the glue sets, remove everything from the lathe. Apply a fillet of epoxy where the waste block meets the reference plate and where the shoulder of the Morse taper contacts the waste block. After the epoxy has cured, mount the assembly on the headstock spindle using the Morse taper. Bring up the tailstock to keep it in place, and then true up the outer edge of the disk. Sand off any rough edges and it will be done.

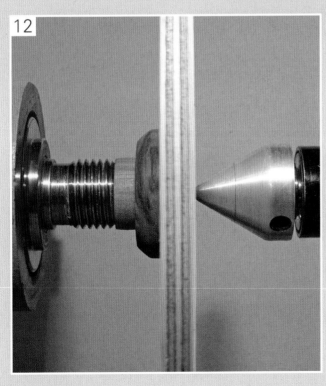

CHAPTER 4

HANDY SHOPMADE CHUCKS

Glued-on Blocks, Small Screw Chucks, and Backing Plates

You can do a lot on the lathe just by using a faceplate or a scroll chuck in a straightforward manner, but they have their limitations. How can you make a platter from a thin blank without wasting part of its thickness for a tenon or recess for a scroll chuck? How can you turn a ring too large for your largest chuck? How can you turn buttons, beads, knobs, and other small objects? This chapter explains how to do these things, with techniques that are easy to understand and accomplish. You can make the fixtures yourself for next to nothing.

In the case of a thin blank for a platter, the obvious solution is to glue additional wood to the blank to seat a faceplate or form a tenon. That is the idea behind glue-on blocks. Small screw chucks held in a scroll chuck can be used to turn small objects. The key to turning a large ring is to mount it on a large disk attached to a faceplate (backing plate). The catch with glue-on blocks is that the gluing surfaces must be dead flat. But that's easy to accomplish.

Single-use chuck. A glued-on block makes an effective holder. Paper in the joint makes the block easy to remove.

Waste Block in Position. Here, a blank for a plate is held with a screw chuck in the headstock. The tailstock applies pressure to the waste block while the glue sets.

Waste Blocks and Glue Blocks

A waste block is a thin disk glued to the foot of a workpiece to form a tenon for the jaws of a chuck or to create a holding surface for a faceplate. After serving its purpose, the block is turned away.

A glue block serves a similar function but is typically much larger and meant to be reused. A glue block is a great time saver when making multiple copies of a turning. Many turners use the terms waste block and glue block interchangably, but I prefer to make a distinction between the two.

A waste block or glue block makes it possible to turn a thin blank—for a tray or platter, for example—without sacrificing part of its thickness to a tenon or to faceplate screws. Also, by distributing the turning

How to Make a Surface Flat

Turning a flat surface is not as easy as you might think. Chances are, the surface will be concave, convex, or even gently waved. I've found that careful use of the turning tools and frequent checking with a straightedge will yield a surface that's nearly dead flat. Shine a flashlight from underneath. That will tell you where the high spots remain.

Use 100-grit sandpaper for the last step in flattening. Wrap a sheet tightly around a piece of plywood and secure it with tacks or staples. Press it against the rotating surface, moving the sandpaper back and forth slowly as the lathe turns. Don't let the sanding board rock or wobble. Some turners prefer to do the sanding with the lathe stationary.

Flatness Check. The shaft of a skew placed against the workpiece will quickly tell you whether the workpiece is flat. Here, the light coming through at the center tells you the piece is still slightly concave.

Turning a Waste Block. The work is jammed between a scroll chuck and the tailstock, then turned with a tenon that the scroll chuck can hold.

The Last Bit to Remove. The waste block is turned down to a small nubbin, which is removed by hand. A void in the glue joint at the center can mean disaster.

forces over a large area, the block gives you a way to hold wood so soft that chuck jaws won't grip it reliably.

Use sound wood for a waste block or glue block. If the block fails, the workpiece will come off the lathe. Any cabinet-grade plywood can be used, but avoid construction grades because they may delaminate. Orient a solid-wood block so that a face-grain side is glued to the workpiece; end grain makes a weak gluing surface.

The glue faces of the block and the workpiece must be flat and free of dirt, oil, or wax, which may cause poor glue adhesion. Sand the gluing surface of the workpiece lightly with 100-grit sandpaper to expose a clean surface. The sidebar on page 52 describes ways to turn a flat surface. When gluing the block in place, use the tailstock like a clamp to apply pressure to the joint while the glue cures. You can also place the turning

on the table of a drill press, raise the table until the block presses against the chuck, then lock the table in place.

When making a waste block, be sure it has a shoulder for the chuck jaws to butt against. If the block isn't too thick, the face of the workpiece will provide the shoulder. Otherwise, turn a tenon on the block itself.

You can make a waste block quickly: Use the tailstock to jam a rough-cut disk against the scroll-chuck jaws. Turn it round and, if necessary, give it a tenon. You can then mount the block in the scroll chuck and reduce the thickness, if you wish. A thin waste block keeps the work close to the headstock, minimizing vibration and chatter. It also leaves a shorter nubbin (and one less likely to break) when the waste block is removed.

When preparing a waste block, be sure that both the block and the workpiece are flat in the center—not concave. Even a slight depression in the center can make the glue joint weak in a critical area. Here's why:

In order to remove the waste block, you have to reverse the turning. If you use the technique of jam-chucking, the tailstock live center presses against the waste block to hold the turning in place against the jam chuck. Then you turn the waste block down to a small nubbin that's removed once the piece is off the lathe.

A void in the glue joint at the center of the waste block may cause the nubbin to break away prematurely, leaving the workpiece

Paper Joint. A piece of newsprint or brown kraft paper between the workpiece and a glue block makes it easy to separate the two when the turning is completed (see inset). The excess paper and dried glue can be quickly sanded away.

unsupported. Keep this in mind when removing a waste block and leave a nubbin somewhat larger than you would ordinarily. You can skirt this issue if you use Cole jaws or a vacuum chuck; they don't require tailstock pressure to hold the work.

A turning is usually separated from a glue block while it is still mounted on the headstock. Use a parting tool to cut most of the way through the joint. Then, with the lathe turned off, finish the cut with a handsaw. Once the turning is free, reverse it using a jam chuck, Cole jaws, or vacuum chuck to finish the foot.

Another way to attach the workpiece to a glue block makes it easy to separate the two when you've finished the turning. Sandwich a piece of newsprint or grocery-bag paper between the glue surfaces after you have coated them with wood glue. Clamp the pieces until the glue sets. The paper weakens the joint just enough so that you can pop off the glue block with a sharp blow applied to a chisel held on the glue line.

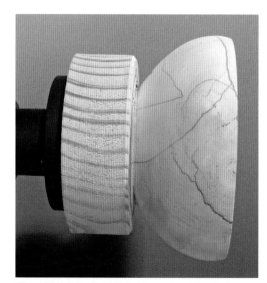

Glue Block in Position. Here, I've attached a glue block to a small bowl made of spalted wood. A scroll chuck probably wouldn't hold the degraded wood securely. Once hollowed, the bowl will be separated from the block and reverse-chucked to finish the foot.

A Screw Chuck for Beads and Buttons

For my bead- and button-holding screw chuck, I used a 10-24 machine screw. Make it self-tapping; cut a V-shaped slot partway down one side with a Dremel disk grinder. Use a smaller-diameter screw if you want the beads and buttons to have a smaller hole.

To make the chuck, prepare a blank about 2½" (64mm) in diameter and at least 1¼" (38mm) thick, using any convenient hardwood. Jam the blank against the jaws of the chuck, turn it to round, and form a tenon on the tailstock side of the disk.

Mount the tenon in a scroll chuck. Form another tenon, then drill a clearance hole at the center for the head of the screw you intend to use. The depth of this hole will determine how much the screw extends beyond the face on the other side of the blank. (The amount the screw should extend depends on the items you plan to turn. Thin buttons can use a short extension, but a longer screw gives better alignment for long slender beads. Ideally, the screw should not protrude past the tailstock end of the blank, but there's no harm if it does.)

Reverse the blank, and then use a Jacobs chuck to drill the pilot hole for the screw. Install the screw and cover the head with epoxy.

Drill a pilot hole through the blank for the bead or button you plan to turn. The best diameter depends on the wood; harder woods require a larger pilot hole. Don't be afraid to experiment. You should be able to thread the blank onto the screw or remove it fairly easily by hand, yet still have the fit tight enough to hold the blank in place. (If a bead gets stuck on the screw, wrap a section of a rubber glove around it and then give it a good twist. Chances are it will come loose.)

Begin with a ⁵⁄₃₂" (4mm) bit for a soft wood and an ¹¹⁄₆₄" (5mm) bit for a harder wood. You can fine-tune the pilot hole with number drills from #18 to #22, which span the range from 0.157 to 0.169" (3.99 to 4.29 mm). If you want to make beads with a much smaller center hole, see page 80 to see how to make a mandrel to hold the work.

To turn a button: do one side; remove and reverse the blank; turn the other side. Don't worry if the tip of a gouge accidentally contacts the screw. The surface speed of the small-diameter screw is only about 1½ mph (2.3km/h) at 3,000 rpm.

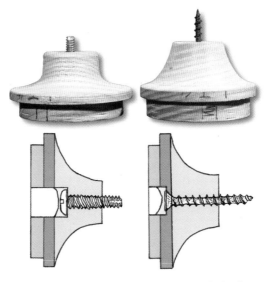

Small Screw Chucks. These fit in a scroll chuck and hold beads, buttons, and knobs. The one on the left uses a 10-24 machine screw; the other, a #6 coarse thread drywall screw. Both are tapered to make it easier to turn next to the screw. The marks on the tenons help reposition the chuck in the scroll chuck. The drawing shows how the screw head is buried in the chuck.

A Screw Chuck for Knobs

The screw in this chuck should be the same size and style used to install the knobs. That way, the same pilot hole that holds the blank on the chuck can be used to mount the knob on a door or drawer.

If you have to make identical knobs, turn a spindle larger than their finished diameter, then cut it into knob-length blanks. You can cut a series of tenons along the spindle so each blank will have a tenon. This yields knobs with end grain on their faces.

If you would rather have side-grain knobs, cut square blanks from flat stock, then use a drill press to make a pilot hole at each center. Improvise a fixture that centers the blanks under the bit. Mount a blank on the screw chuck and turn the knob.

How to Make a Backing Plate

A large backing plate is handy if you must mount a workpiece that is not too tall and cannot be held by more conventional means. It is important for the plate to be securely attached to the headstock spindle. The simplest method is to use a faceplate, but a threaded hub can be made so the backing plate will screw directly onto the headstock spindle. (See page 125.)

I made mine out of ¾" (19mm) MDF. The swing of my lathe is 20"(508mm) so I picked 16" (406mm) for the diameter. The blank was mounted on a 3" (76mm) faceplate using #10 machine screws and nuts to avoid having to rely on screw threads in MDF to secure the disk. The heads of the screws are recessed below the surface on the face of the disk.

The edge of the disk was turned true after the faceplate was attached.

Turning a Knob. With a blank mounted in a scroll chuck and its end turned true, drill a pilot hole for its mounting screw. Then attach the blank to a screw chuck and shape the knob. In the inset photo, the screw chuck is held in a scroll chuck.

Attaching the Work to a Backing Plate

If the workpiece is intended only to be part of a shop fixture and an extra screw hole or two doesn't matter, it can be attached to the backing plate with three or four screws.

Centering the piece is less of an issue if you drill oversized holes for the screws, and then place washers under the screw heads. This permits the piece to be moved a small amount for centering.

Thin spacers can be included under the workpiece to make it stand off from the surface a small amount. This makes it less likely that a cutting tool will make contact with the surface of the backing plate while working the inside corners of the piece.

A different approach is to make holddowns that clamp the workpiece to the backing plate. The holddowns don't have to be elaborate. A screw through the holddown provides the clamping action. It goes without saying that the holddowns should not be installed in such a manner that they interfere with the turning operation, and you should keep in mind that they are there when the lathe is running even though they become almost invisible.

To center the piece, tighten the holddowns just enough to hold the piece in position with the assembly on the lathe. Set up a pointer near the surface to be turned and rotate the piece by hand, noting the runout. Tap the piece to adjust its position until the runout is negligible, then tighten the holddowns. Excessive force is not required.

Cleanup. The ring is reattached to the backing plate so the inside diameter can be trued. Small spacers allow the ring to stand off from the backing plate, to prevent the plate from being gouged inadvertently. The holddowns around the perimeter hold the ring in place.

TURN A PLATE
PROJECT: OR PLATTER

This project lets you practice using glue blocks and waste blocks and produces a handsome, useful turning. However, the blocks are not always required (although I attached one to each side of the thin blank for these photos).

Step one. Install a faceplate or drill a pilot hole for a screw chuck on the side of the blank that will become the top of the finished piece. If the blank is unusually thin, glue a waste block to the top surface to provide a tenon for a scroll chuck or a seat for a faceplate.

Step two. Mount the blank on the lathe and turn the outer portion of the bottom profile. Then prepare a way to reverse the blank. Turn a recess for a scroll chuck or attach a waste block. Mark the center of the foot.

Step three. Reverse the blank and shape the top surface, removing the waste block if need be, as shown in the left photo above. To avoid problems with vibration and chatter, finish the region near the rim before removing a lot of wood from the center of the platter. Center photo shows the plate after the hollowing is complete.

Step four. Reverse chuck to finish the foot. The easiest method is to use Cole jaws if you have a set that will grip the piece. Otherwise, use a jam chuck or a vacuum chuck. Use the mark on the foot to center the piece. Remove any waste block and clean up the foot. The finished plate is shown at right.

The completed platter.

CHAPTER 5

JAM CHUCKS

Workhorses You Can Make Yourself

Jam-chucking is one of the most useful techniques you can master. In earlier chapters, I've briefly explained how it can be used for reverse chucking to finish the foot of a vessel. Now I will describe the method in detail and show how to make jam chucks to hold hollow forms and bowls with a sloping rim, and how to use a jam chuck to true up a rough-turned bowl from green wood that has warped as it dried.

I will also show you how to turn fixtures for the live center that are used in conjunction with a headstock fixture to turn thin disks and other shapes.

Push to hold. A simple jam chuck like the one shown here uses pressure from the tailstock to hold the bowl tight against the flat plate.

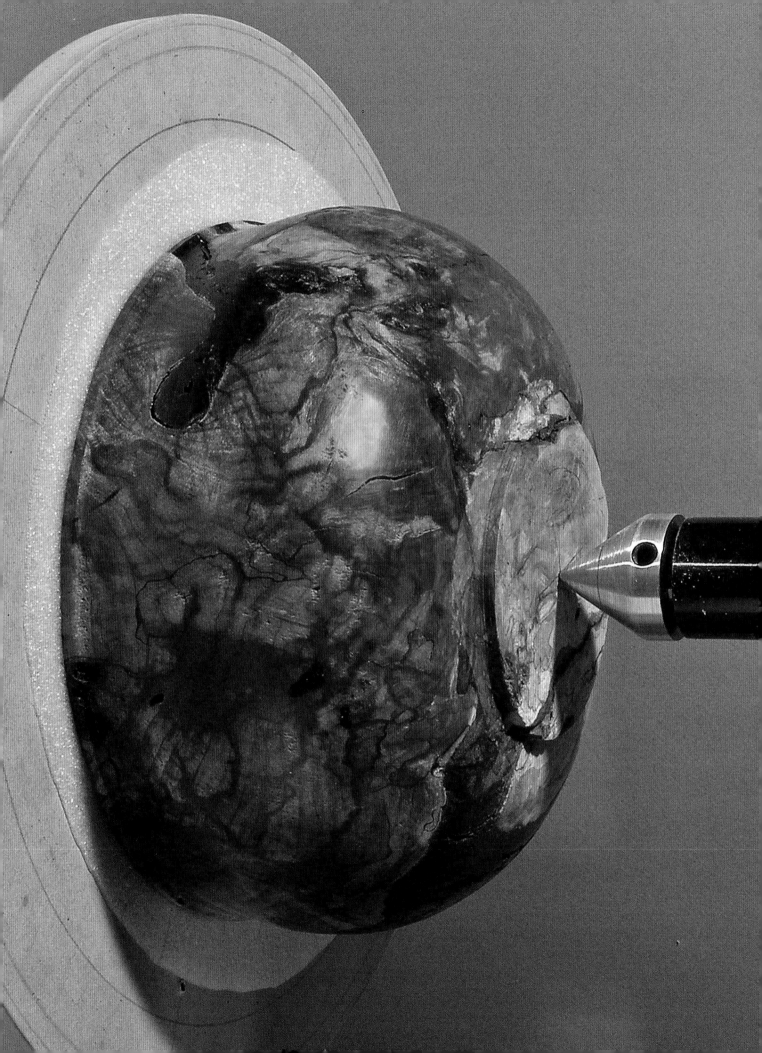

The Concept

In jam-chucking, the live center at the tailstock presses the workpiece against a fixture at the headstock. The jam chuck is the fixture at the headstock.

Make jam chucks as you need them. They can be large or small and take many forms, ranging from a flat surface to one that you have carefully turned to match the contours of a piece. Jam chucks are typically made from scrap lumber, and are held in place with a scroll chuck, a screw chuck, or a faceplate.

You typically jam chuck a workpiece so you can work at the tailstock end. If there is a small bit of runout at the headstock end, it won't matter. This reduces the accuracy required of the jam chuck and allows you to use one in ways that would ordinarily be unacceptable, such as inserting a thin layer of padding between the jam chuck and the workpiece.

Most jam-chucking techniques make it impossible to work the area at the foot's center. So you work as close to the live center as you dare, leaving only a small nubbin for the live center to press against. You remove the nubbin when the work is off the lathe.

How to Center the Foot

Centering a workpiece on a jam chuck will be easier if you mark the center of the foot early on in the turning. If you didn't, don't worry. There are several ways to find the center on the foot of a partially turned piece.

Look for tool marks. Concentric circles made by tool marks may point you to the center.

Use a center finder. Jam-chucking almost always follows a procedure where the piece was mounted in a scroll chuck. So use a center finder (see page 27) to find the center of the tenon and you will have it. You can even use a center finder on a tenon that has gone elliptical, which frequently happens when a green bowl warps as it dries. Position the center finder across the largest and smallest diameters of the ellipse; the intersecting lines will locate the center.

Use a center marker. This accessory, used to locate the center of a faceplate (see page 27), can help pinpoint the center of the tenon. With both the vessel and a scroll chuck off

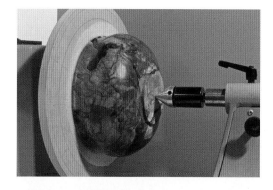

Basic Jam Chuck. The bowl is held, or jammed, between the tailstock and the disk at the headstock. The pressure holds the work securely so that the foot can be finished.

Jam Chuck Sampler. Jam chucks are shop-made, tailored to the needs of a specific turning. These are a few of the ones I've made over the years.

the lathe, reinstall the chuck on the tenon. Insert the center marker into the threaded opening at the rear of the chuck so that the pointer makes contact with the workpiece. Tap the pointer and you'll have the center.

Resort to trial and error. Touch the live center to the piece to hold it; rotate the work by hand and check the runout. Tap or bump the piece in a direction as needed to reduce the runout, then try again. It's possible to center the piece with just a few tries. With each try, the point of the live center will puncture the wood. Too many punctures will make it hard to make small adjustments.

The best method: Plan ahead. Mark the center whenever you rough out a bowl or cut the tenon for a scroll chuck. With the lathe running, touch a pencil to the work near the center, making a bullseye around the center point. Or use a turning tool to make a small dimple at the center. Or bring up the tailstock with a point center in place and bump the bottom of the vessel to make a small dent. Mark the dent to make it easy to find later.

Jam-Chucking Against a Flat Surface

You can use a flat plate to jam chuck a bowl or platter if it has a flat rim that does not turn in or slope outward significantly. The backing plate described in Chapter 4 makes an excellent jam chuck. To protect the rim of the bowl, slip a thin sheet of foam between the workpiece and the plate.

The diameter of the area where the vessel makes contact with the flat surface is important. If it is large compared to the height of the vessel, the vessel will be stable. But if the area is small, a flat surface should not be used because the vessel may slip sideways, get out of balance, and come off the lathe. Typical hollow forms and tall vases are not good candidates for flat-plate jam-chucking.

Custom Inserts for Flat-Plate Jam Chucks

If you often do jam-chucking, consider using inserts for a backing plate instead of making each chuck from scratch. This cuts down the time needed to prepare a jam chuck and reduces the amount of material you need.

The inserts are designed to fit a backing plate with an indexing hole ½" (13mm)

Custom Insert. Bowls shaped like the one shown here need a grooved insert to hold the rim securely. Once the walls of the groove are tapered to match the shape of the bowl, it's jam-chucked in the usual way, as shown below.

in diameter drilled part-way through the center. You can mount the backing plate on a faceplate or scroll chuck, or tap it with a threaded hole (see page 126) so it screws directly onto the headstock spindle. A short dowel inserted into the hole serves as an indexing pin and is used to center an insert custom made for the workpiece.

In most cases, you can make the insert from ¾" (19mm) flat stock. Make a blank the appropriate diameter and thickness. Drill a ½" (13mm) hole part-way through the center of the blank. Fit the blank over the indexing pin, hold it in place with tailstock, and turn it to the desired profile.

You can also substitute a shop-made screw chuck for the backing plate. In this case, thread the blank for the insert onto the screw, then turn it to the desired shape. When you need to use the insert again, just thread it back onto the screw chuck.

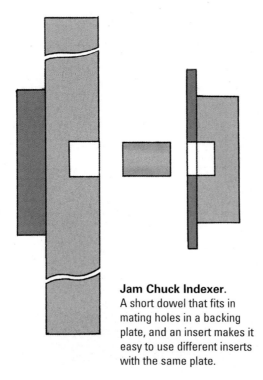

Jam Chuck Indexer.
A short dowel that fits in mating holes in a backing plate, and an insert makes it easy to use different inserts with the same plate.

Jam-Chucking Without the Tailstock

With this technique, you jam the rim of the bowl or vessel against a slightly tapered fixture. Friction alone holds the piece in place. This allows you to work on the entire foot; there's no need to keep the tailstock pressed against the work. However, it's prudent to have the tailstock support the work for all but the very last stages of the finishing cuts.

You can jam the workpiece into a flat plate that has a shallow groove the same diameter as the rim. If the fit seems a bit loose, try rubbing some chalk in the groove, applying a layer of painter's tape, or padding the groove with a layer of paper towel; any of those techniques increases the friction. Instead of using a grooved plate, you can attach a tenon to the plate that's sized to the bowl's rim.

If you're turning a lidded box, you can use the base (held in a scroll chuck) as a jam chuck for the lid. This allows you to refine the profile of the base and lid as a single unit. Keep in mind, though, that this calls for a tight fit between the base and lid, tighter than what you need for the final fit. Adjust the fit after you finish the lid.

Jam-chucking without the tailstock requires some rather precise fitting of the fixture, and you can't take heavy cuts.

Internal Jam Chucks

This widely used technique supports a workpiece on the inside rather than at the rim. It is well-suited for bowls with rims that flare out, natural-edge bowls, and bowls that are simply too large to jam against a flat plate. Typically, you put padding over the jam chuck to avoid marring the inside of the work.

You can mount an internal jam chuck on a scroll chuck, screw chuck, or faceplate. Typically, the chuck must extend farther from the headstock in order to reach inside the workpiece. However, less extension is required if the vessel is large enough to wrap around the chuck holding the fixture. You can buy a spindle extender to move the chuck farther from the headstock, and this will reduce the length required for the jam chuck itself.

The chuck should reach deep into the bowl so that it seats against the bottom or against a relatively flat area near the bottom. The seating area must be wide enough to provide stability so that the rim doesn't tend to wobble when the lathe is running. Whatever you use for the jam chuck, don't seat it against the steep sides of a bowl. The chuck will work like a wedge and could pry the bowl apart.

You can use a vacuum drum chuck with or without the vacuum as an internal jam chuck. Chapter 9 describes several chucks that you may find useful even if you do not have a vacuum system.

How to Finish the Foot of a Hollow Form

A hollow form is a vessel whose rim is small compared to the overall diameter. The opening is typically 2" (50mm) or less and the rim can be solid or marked with voids.

If the hollow form has a solid, substantial rim, the piece can easily be jam-chucked.

Internal Jam Chuck. This cutaway shows how an internal jam chuck supports the work from the inside. It's the best option for work that is too large to jam against a disk or that could be damaged by jamming its rim. Note how the chuck is constructed.

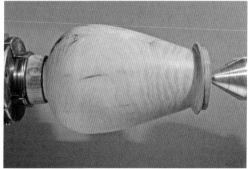

Holding a Hollow Form. A simple jam chuck, sized to the opening in the hollow form, will do the job, provided the workpiece has a substantial rim. As shown in the photo at left, you use the tailstock to support the work while finishing the foot.

Copying a Profile.
Use a woodworker's profile gauge to map the shape of a bowl, then use the gauge to turn a matching profile on a bowl blank being used as a jam chuck. The above left photo shows the rim of a bowl blank turned to match the angle on the gauge. Above right, the bowl blank being used as a jam chuck.

If the vessel's rim is thin and delicate or if it contains voids, the piece will have to be supported on the shoulder surrounding the opening, leaving the rim untouched. The same goes for a hollow form with a nearly flat top; in this case, tailstock pressure can easily crack the piece.

To properly support such pieces, use a jam chuck with a concave center that is deep enough for the rim to fit into. A roughed-out bowl blank works well. True up the rim of the bowl and perhaps cut an appropriate angle at the rim to match the shape of the hollow form. You can usually do this without significantly altering the bowl's shape.

You can use a profile gauge when turning a jam chuck to match the contours of a hollow form or a bowl with an inward-sloping rim. Press the gauge over the rim and shoulder of the piece. As the photos at left show, that produces the contour required for the jam chuck.

The chucking fixture is simply a tenon that fits inside the opening of the vessel. The rim should seat against a shoulder on the tenon. A tapered tenon may pry the rim apart.

Because of the small diameter of the rim and the contact area between the vessel and the chuck, the grip is not well-suited for transferring torque from the chuck to the workpiece. The jam chuck may spin inside the rim and cause the workpiece to slow down or stop rotating when you touch it with a tool.

If that happens, do not just tighten the tailstock because that could damage the piece. Instead, wrap the tenon with a layer or two of painter's tape to tighten the fit. If it still spins, put three or four narrow strips of double-sided tape between the rim and the shoulder of the tenon.

Remounting a Bowl

Suppose you want to put a completed bowl back on the lathe in order to do additional hollowing, change the shape of the foot or rim, or alter the finish in some way. How can you do this if you have already removed the tenon and if the center mark on the bottom of the bowl has been removed?

Use Cole Jaws

If you have a set of Cole jaws large enough to accept the bowl, simply install the bowl, and then bring up a point center on the tailstock to mark the center and provide additional support. You can then form a new tenon if the shape of the bowl will permit that, or you can prepare the foot of the bowl to accept a waste block on which a new tenon will be formed. Either way, the bowl can then be reversed so that additional work can be done on the rim or on the inside.

Make a Dedicated Jam Chuck

With no Cole jaws to center the piece, finding the center becomes the main issue. One method is to make a flat plate jam chuck for this particular task, as follows.

Step one. Attach a ¾" (19mm) plywood disk of suitable diameter to a faceplate and mount it on the lathe. Alternatively, you could screw the sacrificial plywood disk to a backing plate. True up the disk and sand off any sharp corners at the edge.

Step two. Measure the diameter of the rim of the bowl and transfer it to the disk.

Step three. Cut a shallow groove in the disk for the rim of the bowl to fit into. Creep up on the final diameter to be sure the rim of the bowl fits snuggly into the groove, which will center the bowl. The fit does not have to be tight.

Step four. Bring up the tailstock for support, which will mark the center in the process. You can now proceed with adding a tenon or waste block. There is a bit of wisdom implied in these procedures: when completing a bowl, always bring up the tailstock and mark the center of the foot. The mark doesn't have to be large or unduly prominent. If you're clever, you may be able to turn the mark into a feature.

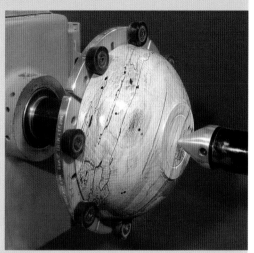

A bowl mounted on Cole jaws with tailstock support.

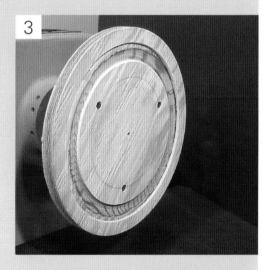

How to Make a Compression (Sandwich) Chuck

How do you turn a disk out of material ¹⁄₁₆" (2mm) thick, such as transparent acrylic?

Make two cylindrical fixtures, one to fit in a scroll chuck and the other for a live center. The fixture for the scroll chuck is simple—a cylinder with a tenon to fit the chuck. The fixture for the tailstock is more complicated; it needs a cavity to fit over the live center. See the project on page 70.

Make the two fixtures but don't turn them to their final diameter. Install the headstock fixture in a scroll chuck and put the other fixture over the live center. Bring the tailstock up and jam them together so they turn as a unit. Now do any necessary clean-up.

Glue padding to the face of each fixture, using silicone glue or contact cement, to keep the acrylic from being scratched. I used thin, supple leather. A thin layer of dense foam will work. Don't worry about cutting it precisely.

Compression Chuck Halves. A compression chuck begins with two identical fixtures jammed together so they can be turned true and to the desired diameter.

Add padding. Glue padding to the face of each fixture, jam them together, and trim off the waste.

After the glue cures, jam the fixtures together and turn the padded faces to the diameter of the acrylic disks you will turn. Use a sharp spindle gouge and take a light cut right at the surface of the wood. Work carefully here because any error will affect the size of the disks you plan to make.

Jam the two fixtures together around the thin material. Turn the sandwich to the desired diameter. A sharp spindle gouge will cut the material nicely if you take very light cuts—a thin wisp of material at each pass.

Insert the Thin Stock. Here, a blank of acrylic is held in the compression chuck, ready to be turned to size.

Finished Product. Two completed disks are balanced on the compression chuck. A third disk is still sandwiched in place.

JAM CHUCK FIXTURES
PROJECT: **FOR THE LIVE CENTER**

It is often useful to make a fixture that fits over the live center and rotates with it. The fixture may be a large cone, a flat disk, a cup center, or one with a unique profile to fit a specific workpiece. For the fixture to run true, it should seat against a shoulder on the live center or, if there's no convenient shoulder, fit closely around the outer edge of the center. You may be able to use Forstner bits to drill a cavity to fit over the live center. Always bore the largest diameter (which is also the shallowest) first to leave solid wood in the center of the hole for the remaining bits to engage. If you can't drill out the fixture, shape the cavity with turning tools.

The instructions explain how to make a fixture to fit a Oneway-style live center that is threaded to accept various accessories. The diameter of the thread on this popular type of center is ¾" (19mm); it has a 1" (25mm) diameter shoulder. You can either bore a cavity for the center, as explained in step three, or tap the fixture so it threads onto the center. That's explained in step five.

If you're making the fixture from an endgrain blank, stabilize the wood by coating the inside of the pilot hole with thin cyanoacrylate and letting it cure completely before cutting the threads. Also, the fixture must seat against the shoulder behind the threads so it will align properly when screwed onto the thread.

Step one. Turn a cylindrical blank between centers. It should be 2¼" (57mm) in diameter and length. Turn tenons on both ends. Remove the blank and mount it in a scroll chuck.

Step two. Square the face of the blank and dimple the center to help start a drill bit. Use a 1" (25mm) Forstner bit to drill a hole ⅛" (3mm) deep.

Live Center Fixtures. The cutaways show jam chuck fixtures designed to fit around different live centers. On cup and cone centers, the fixtures butt against a shoulder on the live center. For the threaded center in the middle, the fixture seats on the shoulder behind the threads.

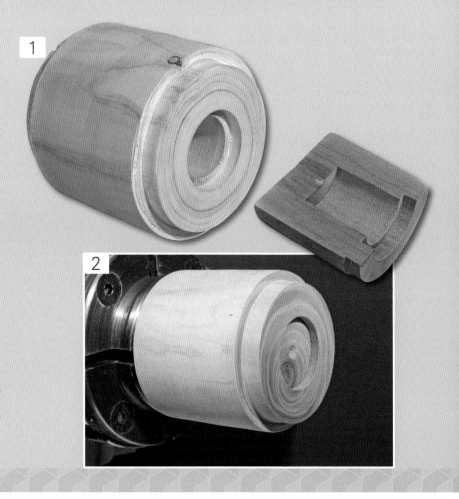

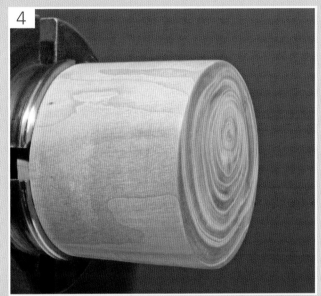

Step three. Use a ¾" (19mm) Forstner bit to drill a hole concentric with the first. Make this hole 1¼" (32mm) deep, measured from the end of the blank. Remove the blank from the chuck and test its fit onto the live center. Be sure it seats squarely and without slop on the shoulder behind the thread without rubbing against the body of the live center.

Step four. Once the fixture fits properly, put it back in the scroll chuck so that the solid face of the blank is exposed. Turn the desired profile on that end.

Step five. As an alternative, tap the fixture to match the ¾ x 10 tpi threads on the live center. Drill a ¾" (16mm) pilot hole about ½" (13mm) deeper than the length of the threads on the center. Lock the headstock. Position the tap (which should be a bottom tap) in the pilot hole, and use the tailstock cone center to line it up. Turn the tap while maintaining pressure against it with the tailstock. Back the tap off frequently to clear dust and chips.

CHAPTER 6

COLLETS AND MANDRELS
Specialized Holders for Small Workpieces

Conventional scroll chucks are limited in their ability to grip skinny rods or dowels and very short tenons. A collet chuck is ideally suited for these tasks, however. For example, the precisely machined jaws of a commercial collet can hold a tenon only ⅛" (3mm) long and perhaps only ¼" (6mm) in diameter. If you don't need that kind of precision, you can easily make your own collet chuck.

A mandrel is basically a shaft that fits into a hole in the workpiece. Mandrels take many forms. Perhaps the most common are those used by pen-turners. Shop-made mandrels are usually turned from spindle stock as needed for a specific purpose, such as making thin polyethylene washers or making beads for a necklace or bracelet. A variation of the mandrel is the pin chuck, which uses a small pin to lock the workpiece in place on a steel rod.

Screwed in place. A mandrel like the threaded one here fits in a small hole in the workpiece. A collet works like a drill chuck to grip the outside of a small workpiece.

Metal Collets. Made by the Beall Tool Company, these interchangeable collets fit into a fixture that mounts on the headstock spindle. Collets like these are accurate but expensive.

Collet Chucks

A collet chuck will grip a piece only a fraction of an inch in diameter, usually without marring the surface. It is ideally suited for gripping tenons on small parts such as knobs and finials.

As the photo at left shows, a commercial collet chuck is very similar to the collet on a router. The chuck consists of the body, the collet, and the nose nut. Radial cuts in the collet allow it to be compressed around the workpiece. The exterior of the collet is tapered to fit a matching taper on the inside of the body. The nose nut presses the collet into the taper and compresses it around the workpiece. On some commercial collets, the body screws onto the headstock spindle; on others, the body mounts in the headstock's Morse taper.

A given collet can grip only a rather limited range of diameters, so you need several collets to cover the range from ⅛" to ¾" (3mm to 19mm). The collets are rather expensive, so this may be viewed as a disadvantage of the system. Nevertheless, collet chucks are quite useful if you work with small parts and need a precision chuck to hold them.

If you don't need a high level of precision, or if you turn small parts only occasionally, there are free or inexpensive alternatives.

Slot-Cutting Fixture. Made from scrap, this sled steadies a turned collet so slots can be cut in the end. Note that the blank does not touch the surface of the plywood. Later, the center will be drilled and turned to the desired diameter.

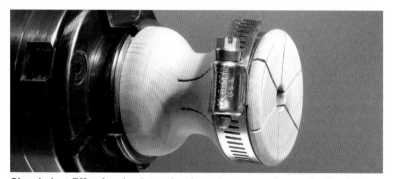

Simple but Effective. It takes only a few minutes to make a collet like the one shown here. The hose clamp takes the place of the nose nut on a metal collet.

Collet in Action. Here, I'm using a collet to grip the tenon on the base of a finial. To steady the tip of the finial, I've jammed a fixture into a small cup center at the tailstock.

MAKE YOUR OWN
PROJECT: COLLET CHUCK

You can make a simple collet chuck and use a hose clamp to tighten it around the workpiece. The method I describe here will work for collets from a fraction of an inch up to about 2½" (64mm) in diameter. The limiting factor is the size of spindle stock you have. A larger collet can be made using a PVC coupler (see page 76).

For a collet with a large opening and relatively thin side wall, bore out the center, use a scraper or gouge to clean up and enlarge the opening if necessary, then cut the slots. For a collet with a small opening, it doesn't really matter whether you drill the hole or cut the slots first.

When you attach the hose clamp, for safety's sake be sure the free end of the band trails behind as it rotates. You can also put a strip of tape or a large rubber band around the hose clamp to hold down that free end.

Step one. Turn a 2½" (64mm)-long hardwood spindle to about 2" (51mm) in diameter. Form a tenon on one end. Mount the piece in a scroll chuck and square the end. Make a small dimple at the center to guide the drill bit used to drill the hole in the center.

Step two. Drill a hole to accommodate the workpiece, perhaps ⅜" (10mm) in diameter. Make the hole about 1¾" (44mm) deep. Change to a smaller bit, perhaps ⁵⁄₁₆" (8mm) and extend the hole all the way through the blank. The smaller hole allows you to use a knockout rod to eject a piece if it gets stuck in the collet.

Step three. Decide on the number of jaws you want, perhaps eight, and mark their locations on the end of the blank. Continue the lines down the side. Cut the slots, using either a fine-tooth handsaw or a bandsaw.

Step four. Put the blank back on the lathe and turn the profile. Cut a flat-bottomed groove for the spiral clamp, and then reduce the diameter closer to the chuck jaws. You want the wall thin enough so the collet can be compressed easily. When you fit the collet in a scroll chuck for use, push a cone center on the tailstock into the opening to help align the collet in the chuck.

PROJECT: **MAKE A PVC COLLET**

A collet doesn't have to be made from metal or wood. You can use plastic—specifically, a plumbing part known as a PVC coupler. It's widely available at hardware stores and home centers, in sizes ranging from ½" (13mm) to 4" (102mm) in diameter, or larger. For larger collets, I use the couplers instead of spindle stock.

Construction is straightforward. Attach the coupler to a base plate, and hold it on the lathe with a screw chuck or a scroll chuck. Or, you can thread the base plate so it mounts directly onto the headstock spindle.

Step one. Drill a pilot hole in the blank for the base and mount it on a screw chuck. True it up and turn it to a diameter about ¾" (19mm) larger than the outside diameter of the coupler.

Step two. Cut a slot in the base to match the diameter of the coupler. Make the slot about ⅜" (10mm) deep.

Step three. Mark the slots on the PVC coupler. If the collet is to be used for making a scoop, make the hole to allow the handle to stick out the side. In this photo, the plug jammed into the end provides a backing for the spade bit I used to cut that hole. Note that the hole is centered on a slot.

Step four. Cut the slots; make them from one-half to three-fourths the length of the coupler. I used a hacksaw to avoid the possibility of getting chatter, or worse, with a band saw. Clean up any roughness from sawing the slots with coarse sandpaper, then epoxy the coupler into the slot in the base. Caution: do not attempt to do any turning on the PVC after you have cut the slots; the sections aren't strong enough to support the cuts. Slide a hose clamp over the coupler and you will be done.

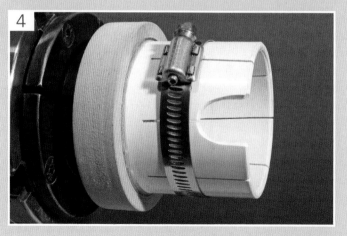

Use a Jacobs Chuck as a Collet Chuck

The Jacobs chuck used for holding drill bits at the tailstock can be slipped into the headstock spindle to serve as a collet chuck. Although simple and quick, this has its limitations: Because a Jacobs chuck has only three jaws, it tends to dent the workpiece rather badly. Most Jacobs chucks have a maximum opening of ½" (13mm), which may not be enough to serve your needs.

There's a safety factor to consider. Vibration tends to loosen the chuck in the Morse taper. The chuck can come whirling out, bringing the workpiece with it. If you use a Jacobs chuck as a collet chuck, be sure it's secured, either by tailstock pressure against the workpiece or by using a drawbar to hold it in place.

The small end of the Morse taper on most Jacobs chucks has a small hole tapped for ¼"-20 threads. You can screw a length of threaded rod into the hole to make a drawbar for the chuck.

Make the rod long enough to fit all the way through the headstock so you can tighten a nut against the handwheel on the outboard end. Instead of using a standard nut and washer, which would not center the threaded rod, I made a hardwood "nut" with a tenon that slides into the hole in the handwheel. I cut the threads with a standard machinist's tap.

To cut the threads, drill a ¹³⁄₆₄" (5mm) pilot hole (for ¼" [6mm] threads). Then, holding

Alternative Collet. A Jacobs chuck makes a good collet in a pinch, although the jaws will tend to dent the work. A collet leaves no marks.

the tap wrench by hand, turn the tap into the hole, advancing it about a third of a turn, then backing off a bit and advancing again. Apply modest pressure to the tap as you advance. Work only from one side of the piece; you cannot cut half the threads from one side and then switch to the other. Put a bit of light oil or wax on the threaded rod, then screw on the nut.

Safety Addition. When using a Jacobs chuck in the headstock, add a drawbar to the end of the Morse taper, to prevent the chuck from loosening as the lathe turns. The turned nut at the end tightens against the handwheel to hold the chuck tightly, as shown in the photo above.

Mandrels

A mandrel is a rod or shaft that passes into or all the way through a workpiece to support it while it is being turned. You use a mandrel to turn pens, letter openers, key rings, and other small, tubular objects. I used a mandrel to turn some polyethylene washers and a wooden hose barb for a vacuum system.

You can buy mandrels for specific purposes, such as for turning bottle stoppers or pens, but it is often helpful to make your own as you need them. They may be supported on one or both ends. You can make them for larger objects, using hardwood and holding the mandrel in a chuck or on a faceplate.

When using a double-ended mandrel—for pen-turning, say—don't tighten the tailstock too much. That may cause the shaft of the mandrel to bend, which will make your turning out of round. In the extreme, you could put a permanent bend in the mandrel.

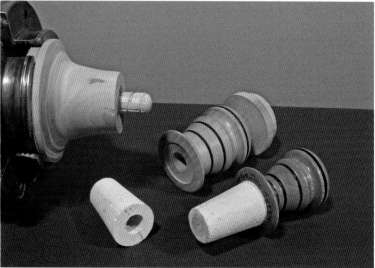

Two Mandrels. At top, a threaded pin at the end of the fixture in the scroll chuck is a single-ended, threaded mandrel. It is used to turn a bottle stopper that uses a threaded insert. Above, a hardwood dowel glued into a similar fixture; it is a mandrel for holding unthreaded stoppers.

Pen Mandrel. Pen-turning relies on a double-ended mandrel to hold the two halves of the pen body. Metal bushings separate the pieces and also provide a gauge for the finished diameter. The brass lock nut keeps everything in place.

PROJECT: **A SPHERICAL SCOOP**

A scoop with a hollow hemisphere for a cup involves some clever turning. It's an example of multiaxis turning; you turn the handle between centers, then flip the workpiece 90 degrees to shape the cup. Make a collet to hold the cup so it can be hollowed.

Step one. Determine the size of the scoop. The swing of your lathe will set the limit on the size of the handle for a large scoop. Settle on a size for the cup, keeping in mind that you have to mount it in a collet later. Mount the stock between centers to shape the handle and the outside of the cup.

The handle and sphere for the cup are turned between centers. Then the cup is held by a collet for hollowing.

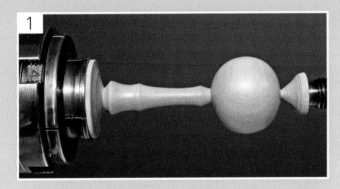

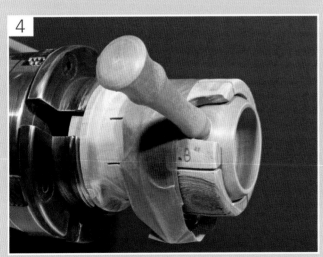

Step two. Follow the procedure described on page 75 to make the collet. While the blank is still solid and held in the chuck, use a hand-held drill to make the hole that will allow the handle to stick out the side. Keep the inside wall straight as you hollow the inside.

Step three. Examine the grain of the cup and decide where you wish the opening to be, then fit the cup into the collet. Move the tool rest out of the way, then rotate the lathe spindle and observe the path of the handle. Position the tool rest for the hollowing. Before you start the lathe, make a strong mental note as to where the handle will be. Use the tool rest as a fence between you and the whirling handle, and do not cross that fence! If you do, you may injure yourself and break the handle.

Step four. Cut a flat surface on the cup to establish the diameter of the rim and the depth of the cup. Hollow the cup. Avoid making the wall of the cup too thin where it meets the handle. That will weaken the attachment point and make it easy to break. Stop and remove the scoop periodically to check the wall thickness. You can recenter it by tapping the rim until it is flush with the ends of the jaws of the collet. Once you have hollowed and sanded the cup, your scoop will be complete except for whatever finish you wish to apply.

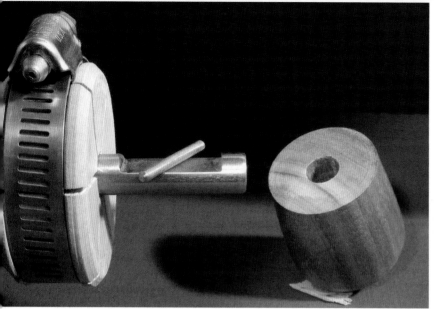

Pin-Chuck Components. In this variation on a mandrel, a small pin, captured in a flat on a metal mandrel, serves to wedge the workpiece in place as it spins. This pin chuck uses a rod ⅜" (9 mm) in diameter, with a flat that is 0.1" (2.5mm) deep. The pin diameter is 0.103".

A Drill Bit as a Mandrel

While making the buttons for the Longworth chuck described in chapter 7, I realized that I had forgotten to bore holes in the tops to capture the heads of the bolts that pass through the buttons. I had already tapered the buttons and drilled the hole for the bolt shank, so a shopmade collet was my best option for remounting the buttons on the lathe. To center each button precisely, I mounted a drill bit in a Jacobs chuck to use as a mandrel. With the button on the mandrel, I tapped it into the collet and tightened the clamp. Once I removed the mandrel, I bored the hole.

Improvised mandrel. In order to enlarge part of a hole in a small button that had already been turned, I used a drill bit as a mandrel to center the button as I inserted it into a collet.

A Mandrel Variation: The Pin Chuck

A pin chuck is just slightly more than a steel rod held in a collet chuck and inserted into a matching hole in the workpiece. A second, smaller rod, the pin, locks the workpiece in place. You can use a pin chuck to hold small items such as game calls or bottle stoppers.

Here's how it works. A flat is machined on a short section of the rod near the end inserted into the workpiece. The pin, whose diameter is just slightly greater than the depth of the flat, is placed in the cavity created by the flat and side wall of the hole in the workpiece. The pin makes light contact with the workpiece.

When the workpiece encounters an opposing force, such as pressure from a turning tool, it rotates backwards relative to the rod. The pin in the cavity rolls to the side a small amount, pressing against the interior wall of the workpiece with enough force to lock the workpiece in place.

You can buy a pin chuck, but the selection is limited. You can make one yourself, if you have plenty of time and the patience to cut the flat on the rod. However, a machinist can probably make one in less time than it takes a cup of coffee to cool. That is to say, cultivate the friendship of a local machinist and buy the coffee.

Lathe-Mounted Buffing Wheel

The buffing wheels provided by the Beall Tool Company are usually mounted on a motor dedicated to that purpose. However, it is easy to make a mandrel for mounting one of the wheels on your lathe. This avoids the expense of a motor and also permits buffing at variable speeds. Two versions of the mandrel are described here.

Each wheel consists of a fabric disk mounted on a ⅜"-16 bolt. Accordingly, the mandrel must have a matching thread, which can be an embedded nut or a thread cut directly into the mandrel. Both work equally well.

A lathe-mounted buffing wheel.

Threaded Mandrel

Step one. Mount a spindle blank between centers and form a tenon on one end. The diameter of the blank should be about 2 ¼" (57mm). Its length will determine how much the wheel is offset from the chuck jaws, which you get to choose.

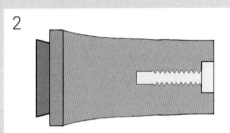

Step two. Mount the blank in a scroll chuck. True it up and shape the profile. The diameter where the mandrel contacts the fabric disk should be 1.875" (48mm) or larger.

Step three. Drill a center hole ¾" (19mm) in diameter to a depth of about ⅜" (9mm) to provide clearance for the nut on the wheel. Then, use a 5⁄16" (8mm) bit to extend the hole to a depth of at least 1 ½" (38mm).

Step four. Use a ⅜"-16 tap to cut the threads that will engage the bolt on the wheel. Apply a bit of paste wax to the bolt for smoother operation. Apply the finish of your choice and the mandrel will be ready to use.

Mandrel with Embedded Nut

Step one. Mount a 2 ½" (64mm) diameter blank that is 2 ½" long between centers. Form a tenon at each end.

Step two. Install the blank in a scroll chuck. Drill a ¾" (19mm) hole, 5⁄16" (8mm) deep. Extend this hole by drilling a ⅜" hole to a depth of 1 ¼" (32mm) deep, measured from the face of the blank.

Step three. Reverse the blank in the chuck. Drill a ¾" (19mm) hole 1" (25mm) deep. Extend this hole by drilling a 5⁄8" (16mm) hole to a depth of 1½" (38mm), measured from the face of the blank.

Step four. Insert a ⅜"-16 bolt through the blank. Thread a nut on the bolt. Drive the nut down into the 5⁄8" (16mm) hole where it should be captured. Remove the bolt.

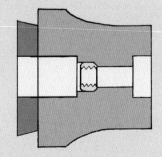

Step five. Mount the blank back on the chuck and shape the profile. Leave at least 1.875" (48mm) diameter at the exposed face to engage the buffing wheel. Test the fit of the wheel on the mandrel.

Step six. Move the mandrel from the chuck. Apply a drop or two of epoxy to the embedded nut. Be careful not to let the epoxy run into the threads. Apply the finish of your choice.

Extended Mandrel

To create an extended mandrel, make the mandrel as described on page 81 but with two exceptions. Do not shape the profile in Step Five. Instead, reverse the blank and shape the exposed tenon so that it will fit into a recess turned into the extender section.

Make the extender section as shown in the diagram above, right. While the extender is still on the lathe, use epoxy to join the mandrel to the extender, using the tailstock to apply clamping pressure. Shape the profile, apply a finish, and it will be complete.

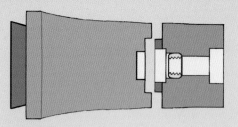

The extender section.

Sanding Pad Holder

A sanding pad mounted on your lathe is handy for a variety of tasks, such as shaping and sanding the profile of a wooden spoon or other irregular objects. It can be held by a simple collet that uses the clamping pressure of a scroll chuck to hold the spindle of the pad securely. It is not hard to make.

Step one. Turn the body of the collet as indicated by the diagram. Drill a hole at its center to match the spindle of the sanding pad. *Note: The spindle may be slightly undersized. For example, a nominal ¼" spindle works better with a 15/64" hole.*

Step two. Use a band saw to make a cut across about ¾ of the diameter. The resulting kerf will allow the collet to compress and grip the spindle.

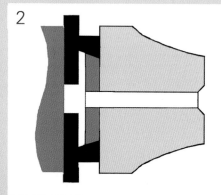

Step three. Mount the collet in your scroll chuck and check to see that the sanding pad is held securely. If it is not, a wider saw kerf may be required. And that's it.

If you have a Beall collet chuck, you probably have already realized that it can be used to mount various items on the headstock spindle. The photo shows a bowl buff held by a Beall collet. It is used to buff the inside of a bowl.

Bead Mandrel

Use a finish nail to make a bead-turning mandrel. Fit a nail into the mandrel base and put a blank with a suitable hole on the nail. A sleeve in the tailstock presses against the bead.

Select a nail corresponding to the size of hole you want in the beads. You will need a drill bit slightly larger than the nail for drilling the blanks and the sleeve, and one slightly smaller for drilling the mounting hole for the nail in the base. The nail I used was 0.094" (2.39mm) in diameter and 1¾" (44mm) long. The drills I used were number drills: a #41 with a diameter of 0.096" (2.44mm), and a #42 with a diameter 0.093" (2.36mm).

Make the base from a short piece of spindle stock, with a tenon for a scroll chuck, then drill the nail hole. Hold it with cyanoacrylate.

To make a sleeve for a live cup center, mount a 1½" (38mm)-long piece of 1" (25mm) spindle stock between centers. Form a tenon to match the opening of the live center. Use the tenon to mount it in a scroll or collet chuck and shape the profile. Bump the end lightly with the point of a live center in the tailstock to make a small dimple for starting the drill. Drill the hole to about 1" (25mm).

To make a sleeve to be steadied by a point center, begin with a 1¼" (32mm) section of a ⅝" (16mm) dowel. Mount the blank in a scroll or collet chuck and square the end. Make a dimple with the point of a live center, then drill the hole, but not all the way through. Reverse the blank in the chuck and drill a shallow hole on the other end to provide a seat for the live center when the sleeve is in use. Reverse the blank again and shape the profile.

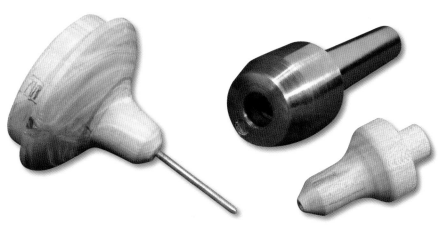

Bead Mandrel. A finish nail glued into a base makes an effective mandrel for turning beads.

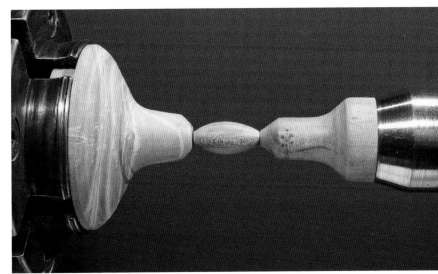

Sleeve Variation 1. You can turn a sleeve that fits inside a tailstock live center to press against the bead blank to hold it on the mandrel.

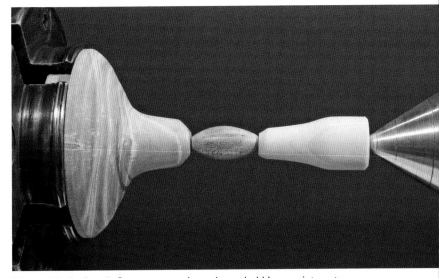

Sleeve Variation 2. Or, you can make a sleeve held by a point center.

PROJECT: **TURN A PEN**

Here is a brief description of the procedure for making a Slimline pen, a popular item for first-time pen turners. The steps are designed to illustrate the basic procedure and to show you what you need to assemble a pen. Specific instructions, although sometimes rather brief, will be included with the pen kit itself. The kit contains the metal parts of the pen, the ink dispenser, and small brass tubes that fit into the center of the pen body. You put the pen together by pressing the parts into the brass tubes inside the body.

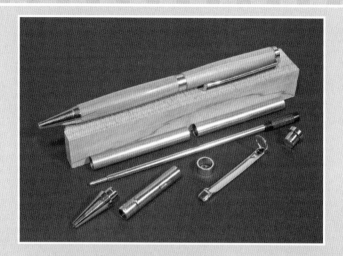

You can do this with a drill press, the tailstock of the lathe, a bench vise, or you can buy a pen press. Considerable force may be required and you must be sure to maintain alignment between the parts; a split may occur if a part is pressed into the tube at an angle. Simple turned fixtures, shown in the photos, simplify the procedure and make the outcome less uncertain.

Step one. Either buy or cut out a blank that's about ¾" (19mm) square and 5" (127mm) long. Cut the blank into two parts, using the brass tubes to establish the length. Each part should be at least ¹⁄₁₆" (2mm) longer than the corresponding brass tube.

Step two. Drill a hole in the center of each blank. The bit required is usually 7mm in diameter, but some kits require an 8 or 10mm bit. Use a jig or a vise to hold the blanks for drilling on a drill press. If you don't have a drill press, mount the blanks in the jaws of a scroll chuck and drill them on the lathe. This jig is for use with a drill press.

Step three. Glue the brass tubes into the blank using epoxy or medium cyanoacrylate glue. An insertion tool makes handling the tubes easier; the photo above shows two shop-made versions. After the glue has dried, use a barrel trimmer (right photo) to square the ends of the blanks and trim them flush with the ends of the brass tubes. You can do this by hand, holding the blank and using a hand-held drill to drive the trimmer.

Step four. Slip the blanks onto the pen mandrel, along with the bushings supplied for the pen kit. Turn the blanks to the desired profile, roughing them round, then taking fine cuts with a skew or detail gouge. Sand the blanks through the grits, typically ending with 600 or 800 grit. Depending on the material, special abrasives are then used to develop the final surface.

Step five. Assemble the pen. Follow the sequence in the instructions for the parts in the kit. For the Slimline, the first step is to press the tip into the end of the bottom tube until it seats against the end of the tube.

Step six. Press the twist mechanism into the other end of the same tube.

Step seven. Press the cap into the top tube. If you are going to install the clip, put it between the cap and the tube. Press the cap in until it seats.

Step eight. The top tube is an easy slip fit over the twist mechanism. It is intended to be removable so the refill can be changed. Place the center band over the twist mechanism, align the grain of the top and bottom tubes, and push the tube into place. The photo shows the completed pen and the fixtures to press the parts together.

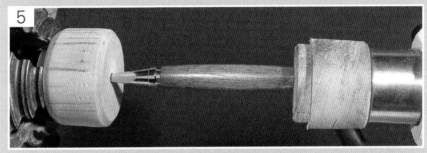

CHAPTER 7

COLE JAWS, DOUGHNUT CHUCKS, LONGWORTH CHUCKS

Big Holders to Grip Big Workpieces

Jam-chucking, covered in chapter 5, isn't the only way to hold a bowl, vase, or platter when it's time to clean up the foot. There are three types of large fixtures designed specifically to hold a workpiece without needing any pressure from the tailstock.

Cole jaws are an accessory for a scroll chuck. Doughnut chucks are strictly shopmade. Longworth chucks are usually shopmade, but a few models are now commercially available.

Building a doughnut chuck is straightforward; all the techniques are covered in earlier chapters. Building the Longworth chuck is a little more complex, mainly because you need to use a router to cut the slots; a simple jig makes this task manageable, however.

> **An adjustable holder.** The doughnut chuck takes its name from the interlocking rings that hold a workpiece at the base. Threaded rods at the headstock pull the doughnuts tight.

Cole Jaws

Cole jaws consist of four flat aluminum plates, mounted on a scroll chuck, to form a flat disk. Rubbery buttons screwed to the plates grip the rim of the piece. A series of holes on the jaws let you move the buttons to grip bowls of different sizes.

Cole jaws attached to a Talon Chuck make it possible to grip a piece up to 8" (203mm) diameter. Oneway's Mega Jumbo Jaws mounted on a Stronghold chuck will hold a piece up to 14" (356mm).

You can speed up the process of unscrewing, moving, and retightening the eight buttons by cutting the long side off an Allen wrench and using it like a screwdriver bit in the chuck of a drill, used as a power screwdriver. Just be careful not to cross-thread the screws.

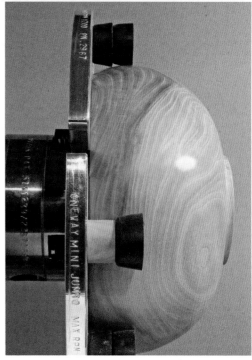

Jaw Modification. When standard Cole-jaw buttons can't grip a bowl securely, try stacking buttons or using hardwood spacers.

Cole jaws don't hold as firmly as a scroll chuck, but they grip well enough to support the work for light finishing cuts. Just be sure to observe the manufacturer's maximum speed specifications. For example, keep the speed below 1,200 rpm with Cole jaws fitted on a Oneway Talon chuck; Oneway Mega Jumbo Jaws should not be used above 800 rpm.

The buttons on Cole jaws work best with bowls that have a straight rim or one that flares outward. But you can sometimes modify the buttons to accommodate bowls with an inward-sloping rim. You can stack pairs of buttons, using longer-than-standard screws. This provides a gripping point 1" (25mm) from the disk. Or, you can turn hardwood spacers to fit under the top buttons. Make the spacers ½" (13mm) thick and ¾" (19mm) in diameter; if necessary, reduce the diameter so the spacers don't touch the workpiece.

Cole Jaws in Use. On the lathe, Cole jaws attached to Mega Jumbo Jaws hold a 9" (229mm) bowl. To the right, a set of jaws mounted on a Oneway Talon chuck.

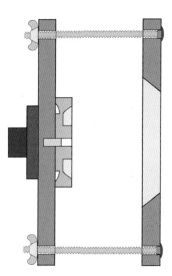

The cross section of doughnut chuck.

Doughnut Chuck in Use. The set of interlocking rings at the tailstock end form the doughnut. Threaded rods connect the doughnut with a back plate to hold the workpiece securely.

A bowl held in a doughnut chuck.

Doughnut Chuck

The doughnut chuck was developed and refined by Jack Straka of Hawaii circa 1970. It is sometimes referred to as a Straka chuck.

A doughnut chuck provides an easy means for reverse chucking a tall bowl, vase, or hollow form if significant turning needs to be done to the foot of the vessel. It consists of a base plate mounted on a faceplate and a ring (the doughnut) that fits over the workpiece. The ring is pulled toward the baseplate by carriage bolts or a threaded rod, capturing the workpiece between the ring and baseplate. Additionally, a centering disk may be provided to serve as a seat for vessels having a small-diameter rim.

MAKE A
PROJECT: DOUGHNUT CHUCK

Step one. Attach a rough-cut disk of ¾" (19mm) plywood or MDF to a faceplate. The diameter may be about 10" (250mm), depending upon your lathe, of course. True up the edge of the disk and then drill a ½" (13mm) hole partway through the center. Draw a reference circle near the edge of the disk for the holes for the bolts or threaded rod.

Step two. Remove the disk from the lathe. Locate the positions of four holes on the reference circle. For ¼"-20 bolts, use a 5⁄16" (8mm) drill bit and drill the holes. (If you're working in the metric system, use comparable measurements for the hardware you are using.)

Step three. Prepare another disk (for the ring) of the same diameter. Using the base plate as a template, mark the locations of the holes for the bolts. Drill the holes using a 5⁄16" (8mm) bit. Also drill a hole at the center of the disk.

Step four. Remove the center of the ring disk. Mount the ring disk on the baseplate. Use thin spacers between the two disks to avoid having turning tools make contact with the baseplate when removing the center. Mark the diameter of the opening you desire, based upon the vessel for which the ring is intended. Cut out the center disk using a spindle detail gouge followed, perhaps, by a parting tool. *Note: Install a Jacobs chuck in the tailstock and use a drill bit that extends into the center hole to prevent the center disk from flying away when it is turned free.*

Step five. After the center is removed, clean up the inside diameter of the ring and form the angle so the ring contacts the vessel more or less parallel to its surface.

Step six. Remove the ring from the baseplate. Find carriage bolts of the proper length, along with wing nuts, and the doughnut chuck will be ready to use.

Using a Threaded Rod

For taller vessels, it may not be possible to find carriage bolts long enough to reach from the ring through the baseplate. In this case, ¼"-20 threaded rod (or the metric equivalent) is a good alternative because it can be cut to whatever length is desired.

The rod can be secured at the ring using either embedded hex nuts or by using T-nuts, as shown in the diagram. For safety, neither the threaded rod nor the nuts should extend above the surface of the ring.

The rod can be secured using either hex nuts or T-nuts.

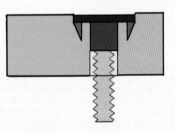

Threaded rod with T-nut.

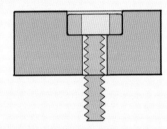

Threaded rod with hex nut.

Centering the Disk (Seat) for a Tall Hollow Form

A tall vessel with a small-diameter rim needs a seat for the rim to fit onto in order to keep the rim centered on the baseplate. The seat should be customized for the vessel being turned. It can be made quickly.

Step one. Jam a disk against the jaws of your chuck and turn it round. Then make an inset tenon on the exposed face of the disk.

Step two. Reverse the disk using the inset tenon. Drill a hole through the center to match the hole at the center of the baseplate (for the indexing pin).

Step three. Shape the seat to fit the rim of the vessel. Install the seat on the baseplate using a short dowel that fits into the indexing hole. You may wish to use a layer of thin foam between the seat and the rim to provide a bit of a cushion.

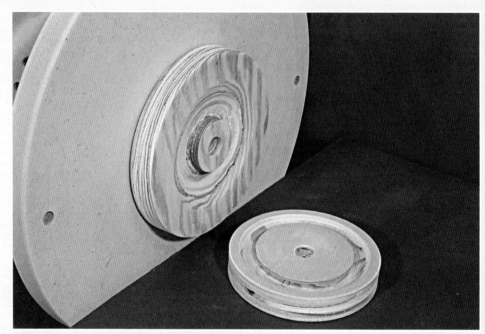

The centering disk mounted on the backing plate.

Make a Ring Using a Backing Plate

If your turning involves a variety of projects, you may sometimes need to turn a ring. A backing plate makes this an easy task. And, of course, a ring for a doughnut chuck can be made using this technique.

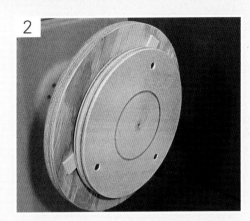

There are at least two methods for holding the blank for the ring (a disk) on the backing plate. One is to use wood screws, but this assumes that screw holes in the finished ring will not matter which is usually the case for a lathe fixture. The other is to use shop-made hold downs to secure the ring. The procedure is straightforward.

Step one. Prepare the disk that will serve as the blank for the ring. Jam it against a flat surface and true it up. If the outer diameter of the ring must be precise, turn it to that diameter and add any details that may be required on the outer diameter.

Step two. Attach the blank to the backing plate using screws or hold downs. *Note: if you are making an interlocking ring for the doughnut chuck described below, orient the disk so you will be able to make the cutout on the inner diameter without having to remove the ring and flip it over.*

Step three. Proceed to remove the center and form the ring. Job done.

Make a Versatile Doughnut Chuck

One of the downsides of using doughnut chucks is that the rings must be tailored closely to the diameter of the workpiece involved. This can often lead to having to make a new ring for a vessel that is not compatible with the rings you already have.

Part of this inconvenience can be avoided by using a series of interlocking rings as the overall ring that holds the workpiece against the backing plate. This method doesn't solve the problem in its entirety, but it at least avoids having to lay out and drill new bolt holes for each new ring. It also allows for using new rings of smaller diameter because only the inner ring has to be made anew.

The diagram shows the construction of the more versatile doughnut ring. It involves nothing more than making rings that fit together. And, of course, it can be simplified by using only an inner and outer ring as opposed to the three shown in the diagram and photo.

Doughnut Chuck Setup

Mounting work in a doughnut chuck is easiest if you begin off the lathe with the back plate horizontal. Fit a short length of dowel into the center hole and press the seat in place. Place thin foam over the seat and place the vessel over it.

Fit together the interlocking rings of the doughnut, with the insert for the vessel in the center. Tape foam padding onto the inner diameter of the insert. Lower the doughnut onto the vessel. Slide the threaded rods through the holes in the base plate and tighten them just enough to hold everything together.

Install the assembly on the lathe and begin the centering process. Pull up the tailstock and use the point center as a reference to help center the vessel. Be sure the doughnut is roughly parallel to the back plate; adjust the wingnuts as necessary. Once the doughnut runs true or with only a slight wobble as you rotate the lathe by hand, tighten the wingnuts until they are almost fully tightened.

To correct alignment if the vessel is off-center, tighten one wingnut to move the vessel toward it while simultaneously loosening the wingnut on the opposite side of the vessel. This should center the vessel in a couple of minutes, provided the seating area is comparatively small and you've used foam padding on the seat. You may need to push thin wedges under the rim of a larger vessel.

Once you have centered the vessel, tighten the wingnuts completely. Tighten the nuts uniformly so that the vessel does not go off center. Bring up the tailstock to support the foot.

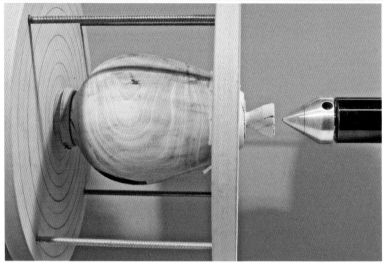

Ready for Centering. Here, the chucked vessel is mounted on the lathe. The next step is to adjust the bolts holding the doughnut to center the vessel.

Ready for Turning. With the vessel centered, all that remains is to clean up the foot of the vessel. Keep the tailstock in place for security; remove it at the end.

Start the lathe at a slow speed. Run it a bit, then turn it off and check to see that everything is still tight and the vessel is still centered. If it is, increase the speed, but don't go higher than about 800 rpm. As you do the turning, watch for any vibration or irregular cutting action that may indicate that something has loosened or that the vessel has gone off center. Use the tailstock live center to provide extra support as much as possible.

Be sure the faceplate is seated firmly on the headstock spindle so that it will not unwind when you turn off the lathe. If it does begin to unwind, let it go. Don't grab it, because the threaded rods—nearly invisible as they spin—will injure your hand.

TURN
PROJECT: A DOUGHNUT

This is a fun project guaranteed to garner comments. Even so, making a doughnut presents a bit of a challenge—namely how to hold it on the lathe for the final, finishing cuts. Perhaps you guessed it: use a doughnut chuck.

Step one. Prepare a blank that is about 4" (100mm) square and 1 ½" (38mm) thick. Drill a hole through its center using a 1 ⅜" (38mm) Forstner bit. Use a band saw to round the blank to a disk.

Step two. Mount the blank on a set of step jaws. Turn it to a diameter of 3 ½" (90mm) and a thickness of 1 ¼" (32mm). Round the outside corners and sand to the final finish.

Step three. Turn away the inside corner that is accessible. Sand. Remove the blank from the chuck.

In order to round the remaining inside corner, the next four steps explain how to make a doughnut chuck to hold the blank so the remaining inside corner can be rounded. This will include a backing plate, a cradle to center the blank, and a clamping ring to hold it in place. See the diagram on page 89 for reference.

1

Step four. For the backing plate, mount a 7" (180mm) disk of either ¾" (19mm) or ½" (13mm) plywood or MDF on the lathe. It can be held either by a faceplate or a glued-on tenon in the manner of a waste block (Reinforce with screws.). Drill a ½" (13mm) hole at the center to accept a short dowel that will center the cradle.

TURN
PROJECT: **A DOUGHNUT**

Step five. For the cradle, jam a 4 ¼" (110mm) disk against the jaws of a chuck (or other flat jam chuck) and form an inset tenon. Reverse the disk and then drill a ½" (13mm) hole at its center. Form a concave groove to accept the blank for the donut.

Step six. For the clamping ring, mount a ¾" (19mm) thick, 7" (180mm) diameter disk of plywood on a backing plate. Form the center hole. Shape the edge to roughly match the surface of the donut as shown in the diagram. Remove the ring from the backing plate.

Step seven. Drill matching holes in the clamping ring and backing plate to accept ¼" (6mm) carriage bolts 3" (76mm) long that will supply the clamping force to secure the doughnut blank in the cradle. This completes the doughnut chuck.

Step eight. Assemble the doughnut chuck and install the donut blank in the cradle. Tighten the clamping ring and then round the remaining corner on the donut. Sand. Apply your finish of choice and the donut will be ready to serve.

Alternative Methods

If you have a small set of Cole jaws, you can avoid having to make the backing plate and cradle in order to round the remaining inside corner. The Cole jaws will center the doughnut blank, but the buttons will not hold the blank securely enough to turn. The clamping ring is still required.

Blank on Cole jaws without clamping ring.

Blank on Cole jaws with clamping ring installed.

Completed doughnut on Cole jaws.

TURN
PROJECT: **A DOUGHNUT** *CONTINUED*

Make a Donut with a Smaller Hole

A slightly different method is required if the hole in the doughnut is too small for step jaws to fit inside as described in Step Two on page 95. Do this instead.

Step one. Do not drill the center hole. Instead, mount the blank on a screw chuck that is about 2" (50mm) diameter. Turn the blank to the desired thickness, then shape the outer profile. Sand. (Note: it's not hard to make a custom screw chuck.)

Step two. Make the cradle (Step Five) to match the profile, as before. A thicker blank may be required.

Step three. Mount the blank in the doughnut chuck. Form the smaller hole by initially drilling, if you choose to do so, and then use turning tools to give it the shape you desire. Reverse the blank in the doughnut chuck as required to do the turning. Sand.

Tip: A doughnut makes a convenient stand for displaying a wooden sphere. Just rest the sphere in the hole of the doughnut and you're good to go.

Adding Sprinkles

Why not take whimsy to the next level and add sprinkles to your wooden doughnut? Turns out, it's not all that hard to do.

Step one. Use an airbrush to fog enough color onto the doughnut to correct any deficiencies in coloration or tone, especially if it is made from dimensional lumber, which is suggested. Brush on a layer or two of lacquer sanding sealer to seal the wood.

Step two. Use acrylic paint to add chocolate or strawberry icing if that is your preference. Let the paint dry thoroughly.

Step three. Apply a heavy coat of Elmer's white glue to the part of the doughnut that is to get the sprinkles. The glue will become clear as it dries. You must work quickly after you apply the glue.

Step four. Apply sprinkles from the grocery store by dropping them into the glue the way you add a "pinch" of salt to a pot of soup. Press down any sprinkles that stand up.

Step five. Add glitter for an extra bit of sparkle. Glitter shakers are available from a dollar store or craft shop. They come in a wide variety of colors with the flakes ranging from very fine to ... somewhat larger. Don't overdo it with the glitter.

Step six. Apply several coats of spray lacquer to bind everything together and to provide a finish for the wood that did not receive the sprinkles. Begin with very light coats so the lacquer doesn't tend to melt the sprinkles. *Note: your finished, sprinkled doughnut will be somewhat fragile, so handle with care. These are not recommended for small children to handle because, first, they will knock the sprinkles off, and, second, they will eat them.*

How to Use Cole Jaws With a Doughnut Chuck

Cole jaws alone don't provide enough grip to hold a tall vessel, but they will if you use them in conjunction with a doughnut chuck. The buttons can either grip the vessel directly or a seat for the rim. All in all, it's a clever combination of the two systems.

I'm grateful to Kevin Neelley for posting this technique on his website (*www.turnedwood.com*) and giving me permission to include it here. Kevin is a member of the American Association of Woodturners, the Kansas City Woodturners Association in Merriam, Kansas, and The Segmented Woodturners Forum (*www.segmentedwoodturners.org*).

All you need is a new base plate, which is simply a disk with a hole that slips over the spindle at the rear of the chuck. Turn the plate to the same diameter as the back plate of the doughnut chuck. Cut out the central hole by mounting this disk on a backing plate with holddowns. Drill the holes for the threaded rods and you're done.

Chuck with Jaws. This thin-walled bowl is mounted in Cole jaws and stabilized by a doughnut chuck.

The Longworth Chuck

A Longworth chuck does essentially the same job as Cole jaws, but it's much more convenient to use because it has a clever way to adjust the gripping diameter of the buttons. Leslie Douglas Longworth, a member of the Hunter Valley Woodturners in Australia, invented the chuck. He died in 1988, shortly after making his invention known to the woodturning community.

The Longworth chuck consists of a backplate mounted on a faceplate with a similar, thinner disk mounted atop it. Slots in the form of opposing arcs are cut into the disks. The bolts holding the buttons pass through the openings where the arcs intersect. The action is somewhat similar to that of a scroll chuck. As you rotate the disks in opposite directions, you either move the bolts farther apart or closer together, but the bolts remain equidistant from the center. Once you have achieved the desired diameter and mounted the workpiece, tighten the bolts to lock the disks together.

For the most part, shaping the disks for a Longworth chuck is fairly straightforward. The same goes for the buttons. The one critical step is using a router to cut the arcs. Complete how-to steps for making the chuck are given on pages 100–101.

You can make the buttons for holding the workpiece whatever shape and size you wish. Mine are about 1" (25mm) in diameter and height. You can wrap the buttons with various materials to cushion the grip.

To maximize the holding capacity of a Longworth chuck, consider making offset buttons. These are small rectangular pieces, notched to accept the rim of the workpiece, as shown in the photo below.

You can mount a workpiece with the chuck installed on the lathe. Hold the rim against the flat face of the chuck, and with your free hand, rotate the disks to move the buttons against the rim. If necessary, you can use the tailstock ram (with no center installed) to help hold the piece in place. Then use both hands to tighten the buttons against the rim. Tightening the bolts on the buttons locks the disks together and tends to increase the grip of the buttons.

After the piece is mounted, rotate it by hand to be sure it is centered properly. Use the point of a live center as a reference to check the centering, then use the live center for additional support until you reach the last stages of finishing the foot. Be sure the faceplate is tight on the spindle. Keep the lathe speed below about 800 rpm.

Longworth Chuck In Use. With a diameter of 16" (406mm), this Longworth chuck can grip bowls that are quite large.

For Big Work. Buttons with an offset allow larger pieces to be installed on the chuck.

MAKE YOUR OWN
PROJECT: LONGWORTH CHUCK

Step one. Cut blanks for two disks, one from ¾" (19mm) MDF or plywood; the other, from ¼" (6mm) plywood. Lightly sand the surfaces of the plywood and seal them with a coat of lacquer sanding sealer. This will yield cleaner cuts with the router.

Step two. Mount a faceplate at the center of the ¾" (19mm) disk. Put it on the lathe and clean up the edge a bit, but don't take it down to the final diameter. Make a small dimple at the center to locate the screw that will hold the two disks together. Jam chuck the ¼" (6mm) disk against the thicker one and clean up the edge. Don't try to match the diameters of the two disks at this point.

Step three. Remove both disks from the lathe. Screw them together at the center with a flathead wood screw about 1" (25mm) long. Drill a pilot hole in the thick disk, drill and countersink a hole in the thin disk, and drive the screw through the thin disk into the thick one. Hold the disks together near the rim with three equally spaced ¾" (19mm) screws about ⅝" (16mm) from the edge. Put the assembly back on the lathe and turn the edges to the final diameter.

Step four. With the disks still on the lathe, turning slowly, make a circle with a diameter about 1" (25mm) greater than the diameter of the faceplate. This circle will indicate the stopping points for the inner ends of the arcs. Make another circle about 1" (25mm) in from the outer edge of the disks to mark the other arc stopping point. Make a third circle midway between these two. Remove the assembly from the lathe.

Step five. Set a compass equal to the radius of the outermost circle. Step the compass around the circle, making distinct points. Draw lines across the disk between points on opposite sides. The intersection of these lines with the middle circle locates the arc pivot points. Set the radius of the compass equal to the distance between a pivot point and the far side of the smallest circle you drew. Draw the arcs to cut with the router. Preserve the setting on the compass.

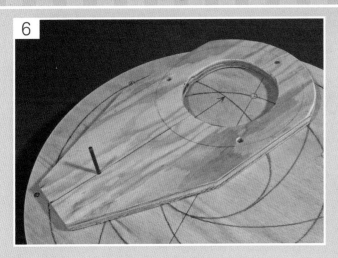

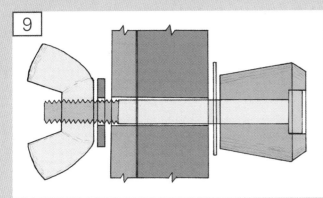

Step six. Make a simple router jig. Use a scrap of ½" (13mm) plywood to make the router jig. Use the router baseplate to locate holes for the screws to hold the router on the jig. Drill and countersink the holes. Temporarily install the router and draw a line around its base. Remove the router; use the line you drew to locate the center point for the router bit. Draw a line through the center point parallel to the jig length. Use the compass to strike a line from the router center point across the jig centerline. This locates the jig's pivot point. Drill a ⅛" (3mm) hole at that point. Cut an opening in the jig for the router bit; reattach the router.

Step seven. Cut the curved slots. Drill ⅛" (3mm) holes at the pivot points on the disk. Use a drill press; these holes must be perpendicular to the face of the disk. Clamp the disk assembly to a workbench, then cut the slots. Assuming that you will use ¼" (6mm) bolts, cut the slots with a ¼" (6mm) spiral upcut bit. As the photo shows, use the ⅛" (3mm) drill bit as the pivot point for the router jig. Make multiple passes instead of trying to cut a slot in one pass. Try not to cut past the inner and outer circles drawn on the disk, because the slots weaken the structure, especially near the faceplate.

Step eight. Separate the disks and drill ¾" (19mm) finger holes near the outer edge of one or both disks to use when adjusting them. Clean up any rough edges on the slots with sandpaper. Turn the thin disk over and reattach it to the thicker one, using the single screw at the center.

Step nine. Turn the buttons. Prepare slightly oversized blanks from spindle stock. Mount a blank in a scroll chuck or shopmade collet, true the ends, and trim to the proper length. Drill the hole that will be used to capture the bolt hex head; drill a ¼" (6mm) hole all the way through the blank. Make a small mandrel to hold the buttons as you turn them. Use a cone center to hold the blank on the mandrel.

Step ten. Install the buttons, using ¼" (6mm) bolts and wingnuts. Polyethylene washers help the buttons move freely in the slots.

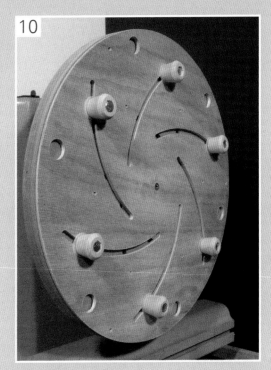

CHAPTER 8

VACUUM CHUCKS AND VACUUM SYSTEMS

Air Pressure Makes a Strong Chuck

Vacuum chucks are a simple and effective alternative to jam-chucking for finishing the foot of a vessel. Vacuum chucks are ideal for mounting bowls with irregular rims, natural edges, or other features that complicate conventional chucking methods. A vacuum chuck does not mark or dent the piece at all. Assembling and using a vacuum chuck is really no big deal, and it does not have to be very expensive.

In this chapter, I begin by explaining how a vacuum is measured and how to calculate the force that a vacuum exerts on a workpiece. Then I show how to build a vacuum system appropriate for a vacuum chuck.

Holding with air. A vacuum hose connects to a coupler on the hand wheel. The vacuum is then transmitted through the headstock spindle to the vacuum chuck. The force of the vacuum can hold even large pieces securely.

CAUTI
This inverte
to be servic
by an
authorize
AMPS
HZ
RPM
CLASS
POLE
DATE
SERIAL
K 001691
WARNING: MOTOR MUST BE GROUNDED IN
ACCORDANCE WITH LOCAL AND NATIONAL ELECTRICAL
CODES TO PREVENT SERIOUS ELECTRICAL SHOCK.
Steel

A major consideration in making a vacuum system is the design of the coupler that connects the vacuum line to the lathe's headstock spindle, allowing the spindle to rotate while the vacuum line remains stationary. I'll show you three different designs, which you can make for less than the price of a pizza. Vacuum chucks are described in chapter 9.

Vacuum chucks have their limitations. They are not meant to hold a piece for aggressive turning. Obviously, you can't mount a piece with holes or voids on a vacuum chuck. And you must use vacuum chucking carefully on large pieces with thin walls; the vacuum can collapse the piece.

Atmospheric Pressure and Vacuum

Atmospheric pressure was originally measured with a mercury barometer: a glass tube, from which the air has been removed, inserted vertically into a cup of mercury.

Atmospheric pressure pushing on the surface of the mercury forces it to flow into the open, bottom end of the tube. The greater the pressure, the higher the mercury rises above the level of the mercury in the cup.

Average atmospheric pressure at sea level is 29.92" of mercury (" Hg), or 75.99 centimeters of mercury (cmHg). The pressure is great enough to force a column of mercury to that height in a barometer. For

Mercury column as a barometer and vacuum gage

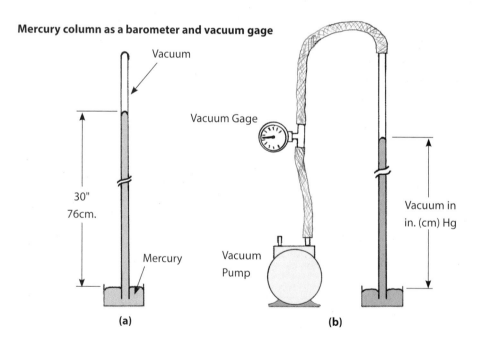

Barometer and Vacuum System. Sketch (a) shows a mercury barometer. Sketch (b) shows how a column of mercury can be used to measure a vacuum. The vacuum gauge gives the same reading as the height to which the mercury rises in the glass tube.

our purposes, we can round off the pressure reading to 30" Hg (76cmHg). Average atmospheric pressure is also often expressed as 14.7 pounds per square inch (psi), which is the same as 101kPa.

You can use a mercury column to measure a vacuum. Simply connect the vacuum line to the top of the glass tube. The greater the vacuum, the higher the mercury column will rise. In a perfect vacuum at sea level, the mercury would rise to a height of 30" (76cm).

A vacuum gauge does the same job as the mercury column. In fact, the scale on many vacuum gauges is calibrated in inches or centimeters of mercury, with 30" Hg (76cmHg) being the maximum. As with the mercury column, the vacuum gauge measures the vacuum relative to atmospheric pressure.

Atmospheric pressure drops with altitude at the rate of about 1" Hg per 1,000 feet, or 8.4 cmHg per 1,000 meters. This reduces the holding power of a vacuum chuck for a given vacuum. But as a rule, you can compensate for the reduced holding power by increasing the area subjected to the vacuum—by increasing the diameter of the chuck, that is. For example, at an elevation of 5,000 feet (1,524m), increasing the diameter of the vacuum chuck by only 10% will compensate for the reduction in atmospheric pressure.

Because no vacuum is perfect, pressure still exists inside the vacuum system because of the air remaining in the system. This is the absolute pressure: the actual pressure in

The Effects of Pressure.
Atmospheric pressure alone collapsed this lacquer-thinner can.

the system without regard to atmospheric pressure. In a perfect vacuum, the absolute pressure would be zero.

A vacuum pump does not reach out and pull air into it. All the pump does is produce a region of low absolute pressure at its intake port. Once that region is established, air in other parts of the system expands into it and flows toward the pump.

Force Produced by a Vacuum Chuck

How much force must a vacuum chuck produce to hold a piece on the lathe? The short answer: about 50 lb. (22.7kg). Many variables come into play, however. A flat-plate chuck requires more force than a drum chuck to provide lateral stability because the drum itself tends to resist sideways movement of the workpiece. The height of the workpiece also matters because of the leverage effect described in Chapter 3. Further, a bevel-rubbing cut puts less strain on the piece than, say, a pull cut made across the foot with the bottom wing of a gouge. A bevel-rubbing cut tends to force the vessel against the chuck.

I tested this with a 5" (127mm) soft-maple bowl 2½" (64mm) tall having a smooth rim seated against a flat-plate chuck. It withstood an aggressive pull cut with a vacuum of only 6" Hg (15cmHg), corresponding to a force of about 60 lb. (27kg). However, it came off the lathe when I reduced the vacuum to 4" Hg (10cmHg), which corresponds to a force of about 40 lb. (18kg). In both instances, I took a much heavier cut than I would ordinarily use to finish the foot of a vessel.

The vacuum readings in my test are only about a third of what you would normally use. Can you apply too much vacuum? Yes, you can collapse the piece if the vacuum chuck is large—8" or 10", say (203 or 254mm)—and if the piece has thin walls. In this case, you should turn the vacuum down. For example, using a 10" (254mm) chuck at a vacuum of only 7" Hg (18cmHg) still produces a force of about 275 lb. (125kg).

The table below allows you to estimate the vacuum required to hold a workpiece on the chuck. For example, if you have a 4" (102mm) chuck, the force produced at 20" Hg (51cmHg) is 124 lb. (56kg). If you reduce the vacuum by half, to 10" Hg (25.5cmHg), you also reduce the force by half. This yields a force of 62 lb. (28kg), to hold a workpiece on a 4" (102mm) chuck. That is greater than the 50-lb. (22.7kg) threshold suggested above, so it should work. You can always increase the vacuum to provide a safety margin, if the workpiece can withstand the additional force.

The table is based on a vacuum level of 20" Hg (51cmHg), which is typical. Here's how to calculate the force exerted on a workpiece at other vacuum levels.

One, select a vacuum reading for which you wish to determine the force. Divide the vacuum reading you selected by 20. Remember the answer.

Two, look at the table and find the force produced at 20" Hg (51cmHg) for the chuck size you plan to use. Multiply this force by the answer obtained in step one. The result is the force exerted by the chuck at the vacuum reading you selected.

Force at 20" Hg (38 cm Hg) Vacuum for Chucks of Various Diameters

Diameter, " (cm)	2	2.5	3	3.5	4	4.5	5	5.5	6	7	8	9	10	11	12
	(5)	(6.4)	(7.6)	(8.9)	(10)	(11.4)	(12.7)	(14)	(15.2)	(17.8)	(20.3)	(22.9)	(25.4)	(28)	(30.5)
Force, lb. (kg)	30.8	48.2	69.5	94.5	124	156	193	233	278	378	494	627	771	933	1110
	(14)	(21.9)	(31.5)	(42.9)	(56.2)	(70.8)	(87.5)	(106)	(126)	(171.5)	(244)	(284.4)	(349.7)	(423.2)	(503.5)

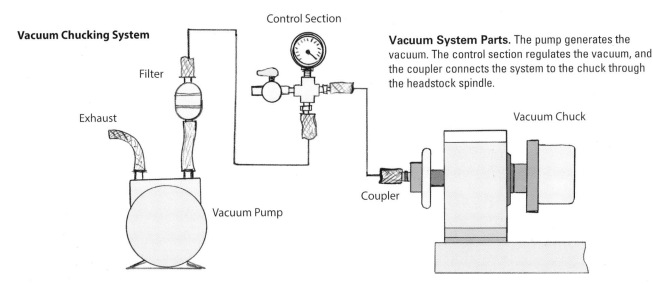

Vacuum Chucking System

Control Section

Filter

Exhaust

Vacuum Pump

Vacuum System Parts. The pump generates the vacuum. The control section regulates the vacuum, and the coupler connects the system to the chuck through the headstock spindle.

Vacuum Chuck

Coupler

The Best Source of a Vacuum

An oil-less, rotating-vane pump that produces a vacuum of 20" Hg (38cmHg) or more is by far the best source of vacuum for woodturning. The system described in this chapter uses a vacuum pump.

Second-best is a vacuum generator that uses a flow of compressed air and a venturi. These units are compact and have no moving parts. A vacuum generator sells for about half the price of a new vacuum pump. However, a vacuum generator requires a large air compressor to deliver a large volume of air at 60 to 70 psi (414 to 483kPa). Vacuum generators are very inefficient but can produce a vacuum up to about 20" Hg (38cmHg) in a tight system.

A shop vacuum makes a poor vacuum source. The reduced airflow through the machine can cause the motor to overheat unless you provide a small opening to allow bleed air into the system. At best, the shop vacuum will produce only about one-fifth the vacuum of a modest vacuum pump.

Designing a Vacuum System

A vacuum chucking system consists of three parts: a pump and filter; a control section; and a coupler and vacuum chuck, which are attached to the lathe. Flexible hose and fittings connect the parts.

The Control Section. The simplest control section consists of a vacuum gauge and a bleed valve. As its name implies, the bleed valve controls the amount of air bleeding into the system. Letting in more air reduces the vacuum. You can also add a throttle valve. It partially restricts the flow of air to the pump, which reduces the vacuum at the gauge and the lathe. Used in conjunction with the bleed valve, the throttle valve makes it easier to adjust the system at low vacuum settings.

You don't need a special vacuum gauge. One with a fitting that has ¼" (6mm) NPT threads will be simpler to install. Small ball valves intended for pneumatic applications are ideal for the bleed and throttle valves. You can buy these and other fittings from The

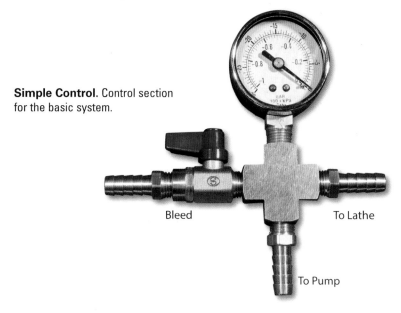

Simple Control. Control section for the basic system.

Bleed

To Lathe

To Pump

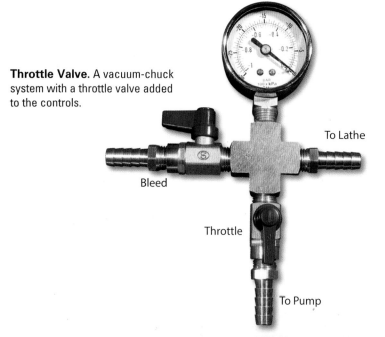

Throttle Valve. A vacuum-chuck system with a throttle valve added to the controls.

Bleed

To Lathe

Throttle

To Pump

Popular Pump. The Gast Model 522 is an ideal pump for a vacuum-chuck system.

Surplus Center, (*www.surpluscenter.com*).

The Pump and Filters. A Gast Model 0522 or similar is the most popular pump. It is available from several suppliers of woodturning tools and equipment. New Gast pumps are expensive, but you can often find good inexpensive ones on the surplus market.

The electrical requirements are simple. Typically, you only have to provide a plug, a cord, and a switch. However, if electrical wiring is not your strong suit, get help. Be sure of what you do in this regard, especially if your pump requires 220/240 volts.

Automotive fuel filters seem to work well for keeping sawdust and shavings out of the system. You can buy filters with ⅜" (9.5mm) hose fittings, which makes them easy to install. Put one filter in line with the input port of the pump. You can also put a filter in line with the output port to keep debris out of the pump when it is idle, but this is not essential. At least a short length of hose should be connected to the output port.

The Coupler and Vacuum Chuck. The vacuum line connects to the outboard end of the headstock spindle through a coupler that allows the spindle to rotate freely. The chuck screws onto the headstock spindle. A hole drilled in the center of the chuck allows air to flow to the pump.

Oneway and Holdfast make couplers, which consist of a hollow threaded rod with a rotating fixture on one end and a fitting for a Morse taper on the other. The rod passes through the headstock spindle and air flows through the rod. However, you can easily make your own coupler. There are several designs described, beginning on page 108.

Hose and Fittings. I prefer to use reinforced vinyl hose with an inside diameter of ⅜" (9.5mm) for the plumbing. The main concern is that the tubing wall be thick enough so that the hose will not collapse under vacuum. This hose slips easily onto ⅜" (9.5mm) hose barbs and usually doesn't need to be clamped.

Small Components. Vacuum gauge, automotive fuel filter, cross, ball valves, and hose barbs.

Should You Add a Reservoir?

If you experience a power failure and loss of vacuum while a workpiece is mounted on a vacuum chuck, the piece will come free before the lathe stops. To keep that from happening, you can add a reservoir to the system. It prevents the vacuum from dropping quickly and helps prevent wide fluctuations in vacuum pressure as you adjust the bleed and throttle valves.

Practically speaking, a vacuum reservoir is not required. You can achieve the same level of protection by using the tailstock to support the work for all but the last few finishing cuts, which you make after moving the tailstock out of the way. The risk of a power failure occurring during this brief period is very small.

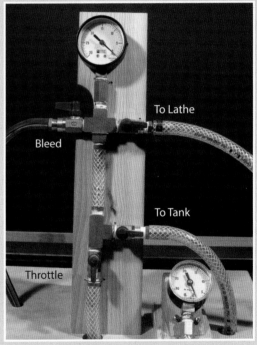

System with reservoir. This is the control section for a system with a vacuum reservoir, or tank. An old propane tank serves the purpose.

How to Assemble the System

Once you have a basic design for your system, plan its physical layout with an eye toward portability and ease of use. In my opinion, the control valve or valves must be anchored to something solid so that you can adjust them with one hand. Be sure you can reach the valves easily when you install a workpiece on the lathe. You need one hand to support the work while you bring up the vacuum to hold it.

I prefer the Teflon tape plumbers use to seal the threads on the fittings. Wrap the tape on the threads so that it tends to tighten as you screw the fitting in place. Use only about three turns of tape. Don't let the tape lap over the end of the fitting. Be neat so the tape stays on the threads all by itself. Do not overtighten the taped fittings. Use a wrench about 6" (152mm) long, and stop when you encounter modest resistance.

Hose clamps usually are not needed for a vacuum system of this type, assuming that the hose fits over hose barbs on the fittings. But if the hose is stressed by a bend or something that might pull it off the barb, add clamps.

Worm-gear hose clamps work well provided you use the proper size and don't overtighten them. A clamp that is too large will not grip the surface of the hose uniformly when closed to near its minimum diameter. You are then likely to get a wrinkle in the hose, creating a leak instead of preventing one.

A shopmade clamp works just as well. Wrap two turns of soft steel wire around the hose. Twist the ends to tighten the wire just enough to slightly deform the surface of the hose.

The Anatomy of Shopmade Couplers

I've made a half-dozen different couplers for my Powermatic and Jet lathes. The heart of a coupler is an inexpensive, double-sealed ball bearing that provides the rotating connection between the vacuum line and the headstock spindle. The bearings I use have an outside diameter of 1¼" (32mm), an inside diameter of ½" (13mm), and a thickness of ⅜" (10mm). They are from the 6201-2RS family of bearings. The McMaster-Carr part number is 5972K42, but I get them from a local supplier.

The vacuum line connects to a hose barb epoxied to the inner race of the bearing. (See sidebar at right.) The outer race is epoxied into a recess in the body of the coupler, which is mounted on the hand wheel. The coupler must make an airtight seal with the spindle shaft or with the handwheel.

The geometry of the handwheel and its attachment to the spindle shaft will determine the best way to mount the coupler. Generally speaking, the outboard face of a hand wheel is either flat or conical, and this dictates the shape the body of the coupler should have. To center a coupler, I use a wooden or metal tube, attached to the body of the coupler, inserted into the bore of the spindle shaft.

You don't need to bolt or screw the coupler to the handwheel. Air pressure will force the two together, and you can design the body of the coupler to maximize the effect. For the couplers described here, it's important to provide adequate support for the vacuum line so that the weight of the hose does not tend to pull the coupler away from the handwheel.

How to Turn a Hose Barb for a Bearing

Step one. Mount a blank about ⅝" (16mm) in diameter and 2" (51mm) long in a scroll chuck. Drill a ¼" (6mm) hole through it. Reduce the end that fits into the bearing to a loose slip fit.

Step two. Make a small mandrel with a ¼" (6mm) tenon about ½" (13mm) long. Slip the bearing end of the barb onto the mandrel

and hold it in place with a cone center on the tailstock.

Step three. Turn the portion that the hose slips over. Give it a smooth, gentle taper so that the hose tightens as it is pushed on. Sand it smooth and coat with sanding sealer.

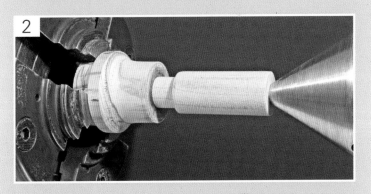

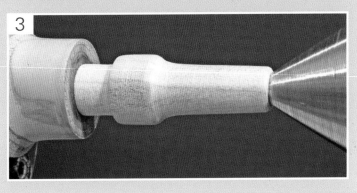

Hose Connections. You can buy a metal hose barb and epoxy it into a bearing (above, top). But a barb turned from a hardwood dowel (above, bottom) works just as well.

You may have air leakage between the bore of the handwheel and the outside of the spindle shaft. The leakage will usually be minimal, especially if the handwheel is threaded, but it may be significant if there is a sloppy fit between handwheel and spindle shaft. Use a bit of silicone caulk or adhesive to achieve a satisfactory seal, or design the coupler so that it seals directly against the spindle shaft.

Constructing these couplers is easy if you form a tenon on each side of the body at the outset. You can then reverse the piece in the chuck at any stage. The tenons need not be removed.

It should be easy to adapt these designs to your lathe, making modifications and improvements as you go. Some turners prefer a bolted-on coupler with a quick disconnect

for the vacuum hose, but I think that only adds complexity and another spot that may leak. In my shop, the coupler is permanently attached to the vacuum hose. Connecting it to the lathe consists simply of placing the coupler on the hand wheel and securing the hose, a 30-second operation if I don't hurry.

Sealing the Coupler Bearing

The seals of the bearings are not perfect. Some will leak, making it impossible to get a vacuum greater than about 20" Hg (38cmHg) with the spindle blocked at the inboard end by a spur drive. However, you can often improve a leaky seal considerably.

To verify that the bearing seal is the problem, try pressing on the seal at various points while watching the vacuum gauge for any change. Coat the seal with a thin layer of petroleum jelly. Start the lathe and let it run at a fairly high speed for a minute or two with the vacuum applied. Slow the lathe to about 500 rpm. While it is still running, apply pressure to the seal of the bearing with the twisted end of a paper towel. I've found this to be quite effective.

Once a bearing makes the seal, it is likely to keep it. In any event, a vacuum of 20" Hg (51cmHg) corresponds to a pressure of 10 psi (69kPa), and this is quite adequate for vacuum chucking.

Coupler in Place. A vacuum coupler installed on my Powermatic lathe. To support the hose, so its weight doesn't weaken the seal at the handwheel, I rigged the support clamped to the lathe motor.

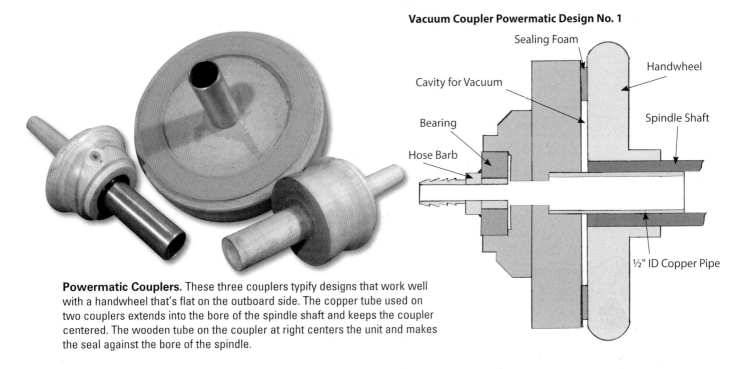

Vacuum Coupler Powermatic Design No. 1

Sealing Foam

Handwheel

Cavity for Vacuum

Spindle Shaft

Bearing

Hose Barb

½" ID Copper Pipe

Powermatic Couplers. These three couplers typify designs that work well with a handwheel that's flat on the outboard side. The copper tube used on two couplers extends into the bore of the spindle shaft and keeps the coupler centered. The wooden tube on the coupler at right centers the unit and makes the seal against the bore of the spindle.

Couplers for the Powermatic

This lathe has a flat handwheel and a spindle bore of ⅝" (16mm). I've come up with three designs described here, which use different materials for the seal between the coupler and handwheel and a couple of options for tubes to center the coupler in the spindle bore.

Design No. 1

As the drawing shows, the body consists of a pair of disks made from MDF or plywood. The larger disk presses against the handwheel with a ring of closed-cell foam sealing the connection. The smaller disk is bored to hold the bearing. The larger disk is drilled to hold a short length of ½" (13mm) inside-diameter copper pipe, which centers the coupler.

Step one. Shape the smaller disk, with a tenon on one side. Glue it to a blank for the larger disk, and turn the two disks to the desired diameter. Glue a waste block to the other face of the larger disk and form a tenon on it.

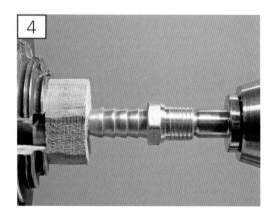

Step two. Mount the assembly on a scroll chuck, with the jaws gripping the waste block. Form the recess for the bearing. Drill a ⅜" (9.5mm) hole at the center of the recess to a depth of about 1¼" (32mm), measured from the face of the disk.

Step three. Reverse the assembly, using the tenon on the smaller disk to hold it in a scroll chuck. Remove the waste block. Bore a ⅝" (16mm) hole at the center for the copper tube. Bore the hole about ½" (13mm) deep, so that this hole joins the smaller one drilled from the other side. Use the point center of the tailstock to square the copper tube to the face of the disk. Wick thin cyanoacrylate glue around the tube to hold it in place, or use epoxy if the fit is loose.

Step four. File down the threads on the hose barb to fit it into the bearing race. Mount the barb on the lathe and hold a sharp file against the threads as the lathe turns at slow speed. Use epoxy to attach the barb to the bearing race and the bearing into the recess on the body of the coupler. Seal the wood or MDF with multiple coats of lacquer sanding sealer or polyurethane.

Step five. Cut a sealing ring from closed-cell foam, making it about ½" (13mm) wide. Glue it to the coupler with medium cyanoacrylate glue, applied sparingly.

Design No. 2

This coupler uses an O-ring as the seal against the end of the spindle shaft. As a result, the turned portion is smaller and easier to make. The disadvantage of this method is that only a small area is exposed to the vacuum, so there can only be a small force (about 3 lb. at 20" Hg) to hold the coupler against the handwheel. Even so, clamping the vacuum hose near the coupler allows it to stay in place.

Vacuum Coupler Powermatic Design No. 2

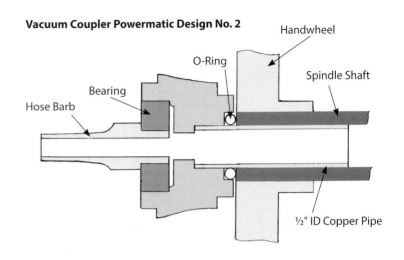

Handwheel

O-Ring

Spindle Shaft

Bearing

Hose Barb

½" ID Copper Pipe

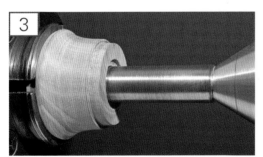

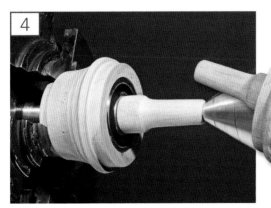

Step one. Turn a piece of spindle stock about 1¼" (32mm) long down to 2" (51mm) in diameter, putting tenons on each end. Drill a ⅜" (9.5mm) hole to a depth of about ¾" (19mm). Form the recess for the bearing.

Step two. Reverse the turning and bore a ⅝"-dia. (16mm) hole ½" (13mm) deep for the copper tube. Turn a shallow groove around that hole to make a seat for the O-ring. Shape the outer profile to your liking, but keep the tenon.

Step three. Glue the copper tube in place. Use a cone center on the tailstock to align the tube.

Step four. Epoxy the hose barb into the bearing's inner race, then glue the bearing into its recess. I turned a wooden barb (see the sidebar on page 111), but you can use a metal barb instead. Just file down the threads, as described on the facing page. Seal the wood with sanding sealer. Slip the O-ring over the tube and fit it in its groove.

Vacuum Coupler Powermatic Design No. 3

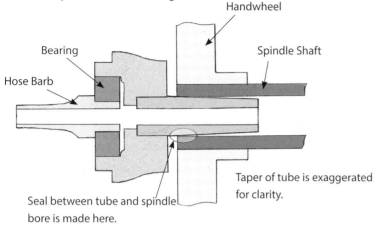

Hose Barb

Bearing

Handwheel

Spindle Shaft

Seal between tube and spindle bore is made here.

Taper of tube is exaggerated for clarity.

Design No. 3

What began as an experiment resulted in the design shown in the drawing at left. The airtight seal is made between the wooden tube and the bore of the spindle. The tube has a very slight taper so that it tightens to seal the connection as it is pressed into the spindle bore. The taper is sized to tighten when the tube is almost fully inserted into the bore, but it doesn't seat with the shoulder against the handwheel or against the end of the spindle.

The end of the spindle bore must be rounded slightly and free of burrs where it contacts the tapered wooden tube. Sand or file the shaft as needed so it won't scratch or cut into the wood when the tube is pressed in place.

In order to retain the natural resiliency of the wood, do not apply finish to the tube that fits into the spindle bore. If, after considerable use, the wood compresses and the fit becomes a bit loose, moisten the wood to bring it back to its original size or even swell it a bit.

Step one. Turn the body of the coupler from hardwood spindle stock 1⅜" (35mm) long, giving it a diameter of about 1¾" (44mm). Form a tenon on each end.

Step two. Drill a ¼" (6mm) hole for airflow through the body and shape the recess for the bearing. Reverse the turning and drill a ⅝" (16mm) hole to a depth of ⅝" (16mm) for the tapered wooden tube.

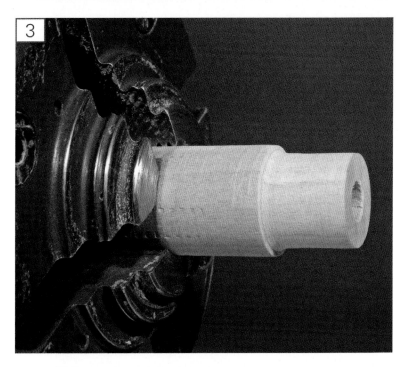

Step three. Install a 2" (51mm) length of ¾" (19mm) dowel in a scroll chuck and drill a ¼" (6mm) hole all the way through. Turn a section at the end of the tube to fit into the hole in the body. Make this section ⅝" (16mm) long.

Step four. Reinstall the body in the chuck. Glue the tube in the hole, using a cone center on the tailstock to align the tube. After the glue sets up, and with the tailstock still in place, square up the end of the body surrounding the tube and begin turning the tube down to its final diameter of (very nearly) ⅝" (16mm). As you approach the final diameter, use 100 or 150-grit sandpaper to form the slightest hint of a taper. Work from the tailstock end toward the body; remove the piece often and test the fit in the bore of the spindle. Stop when all but about ¼" (6mm) of the tube will fit into the spindle bore with a slight tightening when it is pressed into place. Smooth the taper with just a touch of 220 or 320-grit sandpaper.

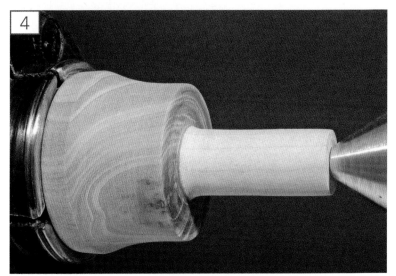

Step five. Make a hose barb (see the sidebar on page 109) and glue it into the bearing's inner race. Glue the bearing into its recess. Seal the end grain with a light application of thin cyanoacrylate glue and coat the remainder of the body with sanding sealer. However, do not apply any finish to the tapered tube.

Jet Mini Couplers. The challenge with these fittings was to get an acceptable seal against the conical handwheel.

Couplers for the Jet Mini

The handwheel is conical and the spindle bore is just over ⅜" (9.5mm) in diameter. Some of the same techniques used to make couplers for the Powermatic also work for the smaller Jet. One coupler uses a ring of closed-cell foam to seal the connection. The other uses a tapered wooden tube to seal against the spindle bore.

Design No. 1

Vacuum Coupler Jet Mini No. 1

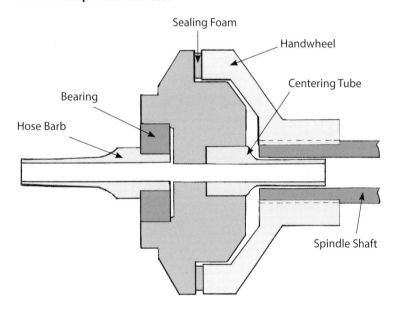

Sealing Foam

Handwheel

Centering Tube

Bearing

Hose Barb

Spindle Shaft

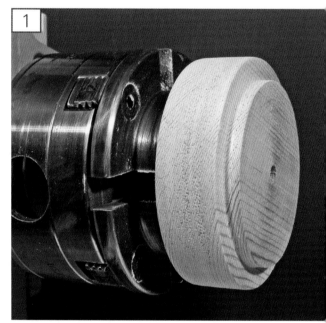

Step one. Make the body of the coupler from any fine-grained wood, using a blank about 1¼" (32mm) thick. Turn the outside diameter to 3.15" (80mm). Shape tenons on each face, one 2" (51mm) in diameter and the other 2½" (64mm). And, as with the other coupler designs, bore a ¼" (6mm) hole through the center.

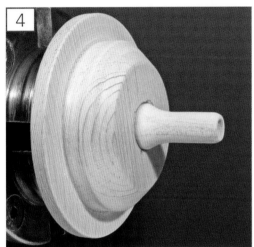

Step two. Install the piece in the chuck with the jaws gripping the larger tenon. Form the recess for the bearing. Cut a wide, shallow bevel near the edge of the blank. Preserve the tenon and shoulder.

Step three. Reverse the blank and bore a ⅝" (16mm) hole ½" (13mm) deep to hold the blank for the tube that will fit inside the spindle bore. Shape the flange for the sealing foam, then turn the profile so that the center portion will fit into the conical handwheel. The flange should seat against the outer rim of the handwheel.

Step four. Epoxy a ⅝" (16mm) dowel 1½" (38mm) long into the tube recess. When the epoxy has cured, drill a ¼" (6mm) hole in the center of the dowel. Then reduce the outside diameter to make a loose fit in the spindle bore. It must not make a seal against the inside of the bore.

Step five. Make a hose barb (see page 111) and glue it into the bearing's inner race. Glue the bearing into its recess in the coupler body.

Step six. Seal the surface of the body with sanding sealer. Cut a ring of closed-cell foam and attach it to the flange so that it seals the connection between the coupler and the flat rim of the handwheel.

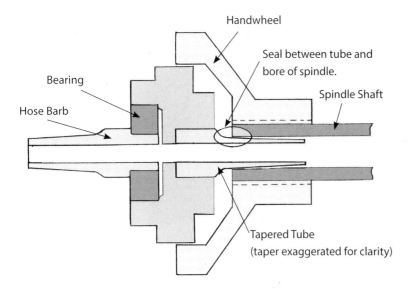

Handwheel

Seal between tube and bore of spindle.

Bearing

Spindle Shaft

Hose Barb

Tapered Tube
(taper exaggerated for clarity)

Design No. 2

Like design No. 3 for the Powermatic, this uses a tapered wooden tube to make a seal against the bore in the headstock spindle. However, the tube has to be rather small to fit the spindle bore. To provide additional support, the body of the coupler should fit closely inside the rim of the handwheel. It's not a jam-fit; rather, the body floats free within the rim so that the tightness of the tapered tube can be adjusted. The tapered tube should extend into the bore about 1" (25mm) overall.

Step one. Make the body from a disk of solid wood or a glued-up blank of MDF or plywood. The thickness of the disk should be about 1⅛" (29mm). Its diameter should be about 2½" (64mm) initially. Form a tenon on each side of the disk; make one 1⅝" (41mm) and the other 2" (51mm). Reduce the diameter of the center section until it will fit with minimal slop inside the rim of the handwheel but still be free to move.

Step two. Install the body in a scroll chuck with the jaws gripping the smaller tenon. Drill a ¼" (6mm) hole through the center. Form the recess for the bearing. Reverse the blank in the chuck. Bore a ⅝" (16mm) hole to a depth of about ½" (13mm).

Step three. Glue a 1¾" (44mm) length of ⅝" (16mm) hardwood dowel into the hole. Drill a ¼" (6mm) hole all the way through the dowel.

Step four. Using a cone center to help support the dowel, reduce the diameter of the dowel and form the taper that will seal against the bore of the spindle. This is a critical step, so work carefully. Remove the piece from the chuck and check the fit often; use the cone center to re-center the workpiece after each check. Use 100 or 150-grit sandpaper to tweak the final fit. If, by chance, you make the tapered tube too small so that the body seats in the rim, cut the tube away and bore out the hole for another try with a new dowel.

Step five. Make a hose barb (see page 111) and glue it into the bearing's inner race. Glue the bearing into its recess in the coupler body. Coat the body and the barb with sanding sealer, but do not put sealer on the part that fits into the bore of the spindle.

CHAPTER 9

VACUUM CHUCKS

What to Buy, What to Make

Once you have a vacuum system and a coupler, all you have to do is thread an appropriate vacuum chuck onto the headstock spindle. The chuck provides both a seating surface for the workpiece and an airtight seal. You can buy vacuum chucks that are ready to use right out of the box, but they are expensive. Some turners complain that they lack versatility. I will show you how to make several types of vacuum chucks, either mounted on a faceplate or threaded to screw directly onto the headstock spindle. I'll also present a few tips for centering a workpiece on the chuck.

A simple vacuum chuck. A disk drilled out at the center is sometimes all the vacuum chuck you need. The white foam provides the seal to make the connection airtight.

Materials for Vacuum Chucks

You can make a vacuum chuck from a good grade of ¾" (19mm) plywood or MDF. You can also use kiln-dried lumber, but it needs to be a fine-grained hardwood such as maple or poplar.

You also need a seal between the chuck and the workpiece. Almost any foam sheet will work provided the surfaces consist of a continuous film. For example, the foam underlayment for engineered hardwood floors is excellent. Many types of wrapping and packaging materials are also suitable. A product widely acclaimed for vacuum chucks is Foamies, a craft foam made by Darice. It is available in craft stores in 9" x 11" (229 x 279mm) sheets, in ¹⁄₁₆" (2mm) and ¼" (6mm) thicknesses.

It's easy enough to mount a vacuum chuck on a small faceplate, but that means dedicating a faceplate for each chuck you make. That's impractical and expensive. The alternative is to buy a spindle tap from the Beall Tool Company (*www.leevalley.com*) so the chucks screw directly onto the spindle. A tap is much less expensive than a single popular faceplate.

Vacuum Chucks.

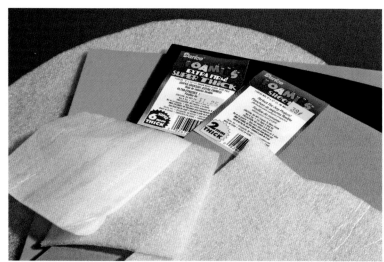

Vacuum Seals. This thin foam, available at most craft stores, is suitable for vacuum seals.

Spindle Taps. These taps make it easy to cut threads in wood or MDF, so you can thread a shop-made chuck or backing plate onto the headstock.

How to Mount a Vacuum Chuck on a Faceplate

Mounting the base of a vacuum chuck on a faceplate is basically the same as mounting a disk for other applications, with one exception. You must provide a seal between the faceplate and the base.

Once you have roughed out the disk for the base, draw a circle on it where the faceplate will go. Drill a center hole, making it just slightly smaller than the bore of the faceplate—⅞" (22mm) for a 1x8 tpi spindle, for example. Seal the surface where the faceplate will be located with at least two coats of sanding sealer or polyurethane. Coat the wall of the center hole with epoxy or medium cyanoacrylate glue.

After the sealer has dried, locate and drill pilot holes for the faceplate screws. Apply a thin layer of silicone caulk to the area where the faceplate will seat. Mount the faceplate and install the assembly on the lathe. True up the edge of the base.

Chances are, the contact between the faceplate hub and the flat front of the headstock spindle will yield an acceptable seal and prevent air from leaking along the threads. If it doesn't, you may need to add a thin gasket. You can use a ring of cardboard cut from a manila file folder and impregnated with petroleum jelly, or a ring of polyethylene cut from a milk jug. The gasket should be thin so the faceplate still seats properly.

Vacuum Chucks with a Threaded Hub

First of all, because of the clearance that must exist between male and female threads, a threaded connection does not automatically produce a precise alignment between the two parts. What is required is a shoulder on one part for the other to butt against.

The threads on a headstock spindle are machined a short distance in front of a flat bearing surface that is square to the axis of the spindle. A chuck or faceplate is screwed onto the threads until the hub butts against this surface. At this point it seats and is pulled into alignment.

When we design a fixture to screw onto the headstock spindle, we must provide a short projection, or hub, that will butt against the bearing surface and provide a definite seating of the fixture. The implication is that, when dealing with ¾" (19mm) MDF or plywood, we will have to attach a small disk to the center of the larger disk. This small disk will become the hub that butts against the bearing surface.

Vacuum Hub. In use, the hub on this vacuum chuck butts against the shoulder on the headstock spindle.

How to Cut Threads
With a Spindle Tap

Step one. Prepare the disk for the chuck base, roughing it to the approximate final diameter. Turn a small disk to serve as the hub, then glue the base to the hub. With the hub held in a scroll chuck, true up the chuck base and make a small dimple in the center.

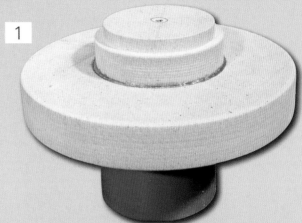

Step two. Drill a pilot hole for the spindle tap, making it ⅛" (3mm) smaller than the spindle thread. So, for a 1¼" (32mm) thread, drill a 1⅛" (29mm)-diameter hole. When you bore the pilot hole, be careful not to punch through and hit the bottoms of the jaws with the bit. Stay back ⅛" (3mm) or so from the rear surface. Cut a slight bevel around the rim of the hole to provide an easy entry for the tap.

Step three. Set up the spindle tap. Turn off the lathe and lock the spindle (if your lathe does not have a spindle lock, use a long-handled wrench clamped to the lathe bed to immobilize the headstock). You can use a box wrench to turn the tap, but I find it easier to use a shopmade tap wrench, as shown in the photo. A ½" (13mm) hole filed square fits over the end of the tap; 3" (76mm)-long spokes epoxied into the disk make it easy to turn. Place the cutting end of the tap loosely in the hole to be threaded, and bring the tailstock cone center up to fit into a small dimple on the end of the tap.

Step four. Assemble the supplies shown in the photo and begin cutting the threads. If you plan to cut threads in end grain or plywood, as shown here, first coat the inside of the pilot hole with thin cyanoacrylate and let it cure for several minutes. After you have cut the threads, give them another coat of thin cyanoacrylate and let it cure for perhaps half an hour. To clean up the threads, squirt them with silicone lubricant and run the tap in again. The best way to cut the threads is to advance the tap, back off, then advance again, going a bit farther than you did before. At the same time, turn the tailstock handwheel to maintain pressure on the tap. This will produce cleaner threads. The back-and-forth cutting technique keeps the tap from locking up inside a partially threaded hole. Keep going back and forth even if the tap advances easily. Keep the chips cleared by blowing air around the tap. If it becomes hard to turn, chances are that the chips need to be cleared.

Step five. Remove the tap after you have cut threads all the way through the vacuum-chuck base and most of the way through the hub. Remove the piece from the scroll chuck and remove the chuck to expose the threads of the headstock spindle. Turn a ring that will serve as a spacer between the face of the disk and the bearing surface of the spindle. Use a scrap of plywood either ⅜" or ½" thick (9.5 or 13mm). Jam the blank against scroll-chuck jaws to true the outside diameter. Then mount it inside the chuck and get it flush with the front of the jaws. Turn away the inside of the ring so that it will slip over the threads on the spindle.

Step six. With the completed ring in place, screw the threaded chuck base onto the spindle and be sure it seats against the ring. Refine the shape of the hub. If you did not bore the pilot hole for the spindle tap all the way through the blank, turn away the waste until the hole opens up, exposing the end of the spindle. Then cut away any threads that are only partially cut near the face of the hub. In the region where the partial threads are removed, turn the diameter to match the outside diameter of the threads on the spindle. You can also shorten the hub if you wish. Coat the threads with sanding sealer.

How to Make a Threaded Backing Plate

Sometimes, all you need to hold work with a vacuum is the chuck base itself, otherwise called a backing plate or a flat-plate vacuum chuck. You make a backing plate essentially the same way you do a chuck base. For the plate, though, reduce the thickness of the hub disk and put a groove in the hub for an O-ring.

Follow the first five steps for cutting threads with a spindle tap (page 126). Then reverse the assembly, screw it onto the headstock spindle, and open up the hole at the center. Reduce the hub thickness so that when it butts against the bearing surface in use, the end of the spindle will be nearly flush with the face of the disk. To determine the amount to remove, measure the distance from the end of the spindle to the face of the hub. Then subtract the thickness of the spacer.

If you've made the plate from MDF, you may want to coat it with sanding sealer before making the final cuts. Turn away any partially cut threads that may remain. Enlarge the internal diameter so that it will slip over the spindle to a point where clean, fully-cut threads are exposed. Cut the groove for the O-ring. Coat the threads and the surface of the backing plate with sanding sealer or polyurethane.

You can simplify the process by eliminating the O-ring. My observation, after working with several different vacuum chucks, is that the O-ring is not needed. Apparently, air leakage past cleanly-cut threads is insignificant, even with the chuck partially unscrewed, which I did to test the seal with a backing plate minus the O-ring. You can add the O-ring later if leakage past the threads turns out to be a problem.

A Gallery of Vacuum Chucks

Using the threaded backing plate as a base, you can make a variety of vacuum chucks for different applications.

Flat-plate chuck

You can mount a bowl with a flat rim on the flat surface of the backing plate with only a gasket between the two. The gasket, cut from a thin sheet of foam, is fastened to the backing plate with a few strips of double-sided tape. Center the vessel over the ring of foam and apply the vacuum.

Concave-plate chuck

You may be tempted to use a flat-plate chuck to hold the flat inside of a large platter so you can finish the bottom of the platter. Unfortunately, that will not work. A flat against a flat is not good because there is no passageway for air except in that small area adjacent to the opening at the headstock spindle. That means no vacuum will be produced over most of the area of contact. There will not be nearly enough force to hold the piece.

For a proper hold, make the backing plate slightly concave. The concavity does not have to be great, perhaps ¼"(6mm) across a diameter of 6"(152mm), but make sure that sealing foam doesn't wander in and fill the space.

Flat Plate Chuck. One of the simplest vacuum chucks. The ring of foam provides the seal.

Drum chuck

A drum chuck is a hollow cylinder mounted on the headstock spindle. Here's how to make one, using a threaded base and a large-diameter PVC coupling.

Make the threaded base about an inch (25mm) greater in diameter than the coupling you intend to use. Mount it on the lathe and cut a ⅜" (9.5mm)-deep groove for the end of the coupling. Provide just enough clearance

Multiple Uses. A small drum chuck made from PVC, with a rim ring epoxied to it. You can use this as a vacuum chuck or an ordinary jam chuck.

PVC Couplings. These stock plumbing parts, available in several diameters, make ideal drum chucks.

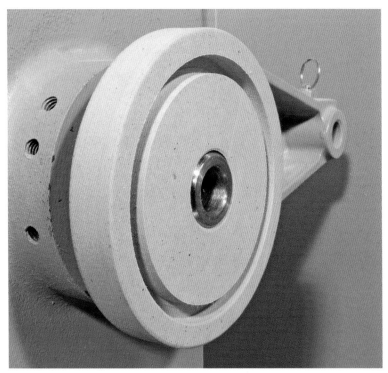

Drum Chuck Base. An MDF backing plate, tapped to thread on the headstock spindle and turned with a groove for the PVC coupling. A bed of epoxy in the bottom of the groove will hold the coupling and prevent air leakage.

between the coupling and the walls of the groove so that epoxy can flow between the two when you press the coupling into the groove.

At this point, prepare to use the tailstock to force the coupling into the groove. You will need a flat disk or small scrap of wood large enough to cover the end of the coupling.

Remove the base from the lathe and put it on a horizontal surface. Spread a bed of epoxy in the bottom of the groove. Then place the coupling in the groove and push it into the epoxy.

Without delay and without letting the coupling come out of the groove, screw the base onto the headstock spindle. Bring up the tailstock and apply pressure to the coupling. Be sure the PVC seats evenly in the groove. Leave it there until the epoxy cures.

After the epoxy has cured and with the tailstock out of the way, rotate the lathe slowly and check for runout at the rim. Hopefully, it will be minimal. It is now time for a critical operation, turning a true, rounded surface on the exposed end of the

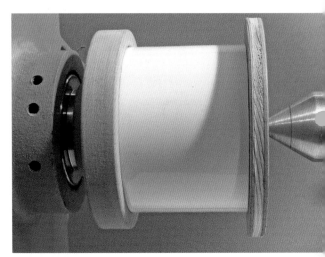

Final Assembly. Pressure from the tailstock helps seat the PVC coupling into the groove.

Drum Chuck. A vacuum drum chuck without a rim ring. The end of the PVC has to be turned true and smoothed.

coupling. PVC turns nicely, but the last thing you want is a catch. Use your sharpest tool and safest cut. Or, you can add a rim ring, as described below.

Coarse steel wool with the lathe turning at a low speed will remove tool marks if they aren't too severe. Burnishing with the shank of a turning tool will make the plastic shine.

You may wish to add a fillet of epoxy around the base of the coupling, inside and outside. Coat the entire base with sanding sealer or epoxy thinned with denatured alcohol.

Rim ring for a drum chuck

With only a ¼" (6mm) wall thickness, the rim of a coupling is fairly sharp and will contact the sealing foam only in a relatively narrow line, which can make a permanent dent in the foam. You may wish to turn a ring to cover the rim and provide a more rounded surface for the workpiece to seat against.

Begin with a solid disk that's about 1"(25mm) larger than the rim of the coupling. Mount the disk on a screw chuck or jam it against the jaws of a scroll chuck. Cut a groove for the rim of the coupling to fit into, as you would for a drum chuck.

Beginning a Rim Ring. After turning a disk to size and cutting a groove for the PVC, epoxy it to the drum and use the tailstock to hold it until the adhesive sets.

Shaping the Rim Ring. With the tailstock steadying the work, cut away the center of the ring and shape the rim. Here, it is at the point where the center is about to break free.

Centering the Workpiece on a Vacuum Chuck

This is similar to centering a workpiece on an ordinary jam chuck, which is described in Chapter 5 on page 62. In that section, I emphasized the importance of marking the center point on the foot. Almost always, centering the work on the lathe is easier if you have marked the center so that a point center on the tailstock can be used to position the work.

When you turn a piece held with a vacuum chuck, keep the tailstock against the work for safety whenever possible. A vacuum chuck does not provide as much resistance to sideways movement of the workpiece as a point center applied to the foot, and in the event you lose the vacuum unexpectedly, the tailstock could save the day.

As you apply the vacuum, the sealing foam will be compressed and the workpiece will move slightly toward the headstock. Pay attention to the point center if you are using it to center the work. Sometimes the movement is enough to disengage the point from the foot of the piece.

Remove the disk from the lathe, spread epoxy in the groove, and push the rim of the coupling into the epoxy. Mount it back on the lathe and use tailstock pressure to hold the disk against the PVC coupling. Let the epoxy cure.

Leave the tailstock in place to support the work and turn the desired profile on the outer portion of the ring. Work as far as you dare toward the inside of the ring, then remove the tailstock. Slow the lathe speed and use a parting tool to separate the center of the disk from the ring. Turn a smooth contour on the inside surface of the ring. Finally, apply multiple coats of a sealer to the entire ring.

If your first try at centering the workpiece results in too much runout, you can reduce the vacuum and bump the piece lightly in the direction it needs to go. Just be careful adjusting the vacuum so you don't accidentally drop the piece off the chuck. This is where the throttle valve in the vacuum-control section comes in handy; it makes the vacuum easy to adjust at low vacuum levels.

Usually the turning step just prior to vacuum chucking is done with the work mounted on a scroll chuck or faceplate. Two tailstock accessories are available that allow you to unscrew the chuck or faceplate with the workpiece still attached, turn it around, and reinstall it on the tailstock. Once the vacuum chuck is installed on the headstock spindle, the tailstock is then used to position the workpiece on the vacuum chuck. This makes it easier to center the work on the vacuum chuck.

Using a Live Center Adaptor. Oneway makes a live center adaptor, which allows a chuck or faceplate to be mounted on the tailstock. The adaptor converts the thread on the Oneway live center to the same thread as the spindle so that a chuck or faceplate can be mounted on the tailstock. This feature can be used to center a workpiece on a vacuum chuck, as explained above. Once the vacuum holds the piece securely, remove the chuck or faceplate and finish with the turning.

Using a Reversing Adaptor. Also known as positioning adaptors, these combine a spindle thread with a Morse taper that can be installed into the tailstock ram. They serve the same purpose as the Oneway live center adaptor, but because the adaptor cannot (or should not) rotate in the Morse taper of the tailstock, the workpiece cannot be rotated during the positioning process.

These adaptors are intended only for positioning, as described here. You must not use the adaptor to mount a chuck or

Live Center Adaptor. The adaptor is the section between the scroll chuck and the tailstock live center. Here, I'm using the adaptor to place a bowl on a vacuum drum chuck.

Reversing Adaptor. The Morse taper spindle fits in the tailstock. You mount a scroll chuck or faceplate on the threaded end.

faceplate onto the headstock spindle because the adaptor may loosen and come out of the Morse taper. It's the same issue that requires a Jacobs chuck used as a collet to be held in place with a drawbar.

A collection of disks
and rings.

Discs and Rings from Thin Materials

Discs and rings made from materials like thin craft foam, polyethylene lids from the kitchen, thin plywood, and even leather have a variety of uses—as seals for vacuum chucks, templates for round or spherical objects, and even items for craft projects. These can be made with precision on a lathe.

Because the materials are not strong enough to be self-supporting, they must be compressed between two rigid surfaces. This is usually accomplished by clamping the material between a flat backing plate and a clamping disk. Clamping pressure is supplied by the tailstock.

The material can be cut easily with the long point of a skew or the sharp point of a detail gouge. The cut is made at the edge of the clamping disc, which, therefore, determines the diameter of the cut.

Backing plate, compression disk, and tailstock.

The position of the skew when making a cut.

Making a Ring

This is a two-step process. The larger diameter is cut first followed by changing to a smaller clamping disk. The cut for the smaller diameter is then made. A means must be provided for holding the thin blank on the backing plate while the clamping disk is changed. This can be done with a small strip of double-sided tape between the material and the backing plate.

To make a template for a sphere, first make a ring whose inner diameter is what is desired for the sphere. Then, cut out a section of the ring to use as the template. It's that simple.

Preparing to make the cut for the inner diameter.

CHAPTER 10

STEADY RESTS
Accessories to Keep the Work in Line

Like any other chuck, a steady rest (or steady) attaches to the lathe and helps stabilize the workpiece while it is being turned. Unlike other chucks, most steady rests ride on the lathe bed instead of the headstock or tailstock. Steady rests are especially useful when turning long spindles, tall vases, and large thin-walled bowls.

For example, suppose you plan to turn a thin candle holder that is about 10" (254mm) tall with the cup for the candle formed at the top end of the spindle. Without a steady rest to stabilize the end of the piece, turning the cup will be an uncertain affair. You will be lucky to do it successfully.

Steady rests take many forms. Some have rollers that contact the workpiece. Others use a web of string to stabilize light, delicate spindles. You can even use a clothespin as a steady rest for a small spindle. Only a limited selection of steady rests are available commercially, so woodturners often make their own, using MDF or plywood and wheels intended for inline skates or scooters.

> **Gentle pressure on a spindle.** The rollers on a steady rest ride against the middle of a spindle to keep it from flexing when you apply pressure with a turning tool.

Vibration, Bending, and Flexing

These troublesome effects arise when the workpiece extends a considerable distance from the headstock or tailstock. They are the result of centrifugal force and the force you exert on the workpiece with turning tools. Wood is not perfectly rigid and it will bend and flex when a force is applied to it. Vibration results when bending and flexing are coupled with the rotation of the piece.

This is easy to demonstrate. Install a piece of spindle stock about 4" (102mm) long and 1" (25mm) in diameter in a chuck; leave the tailstock end of the piece unsupported. Make a cut near the free end with a gouge. You will hear the vibration as the wood flexes under the force of your tool. Now, bring up the live center and use it to stabilize the end of the piece. When you make another cut, the vibration will be gone.

The leverage effect is the dominant issue when hollowing a tall vase, working far from the chuck on an unsupported end. On the other hand, when you are turning a long, skinny spindle at a high lathe speed, the main concern is centrifugal force stemming from unbalanced parts of the piece. In either case, if you don't add additional support to steady the piece, it can be destroyed.

Steadies: From Large to Small

Most of the projects that follow are my adaptations of traditional designs. You'll need to adapt any design to suit your own lathe. In most cases, the dimensions are not critical, but the frame should be centered on the axis of the lathe spindle. An easy way to find the exact distance from the center of the spindle to the top of the ways is to stand a piece of squared, flat stock on the ways and bump it against a point center installed in the tailstock ram. Measure the distance from the squared edge to the point made by the center.

An Internet search for kick-scooter wheels will turn up sources for 100mm replacement wheels with Abec 7 bearings for Razor scooters. The bearings used for the small spindle steady are the same double-sealed bearings used to make vacuum couplers (see page 108).

You must turn a flat area, or track, on the workpiece for the rollers to press against. The track should have as little runout as you can manage. I get the best results by making the final cuts with a square-end scraper. If the track's diameter is larger than that of the rollers, the rollers will turn faster than the lathe speed. To minimize the stress on the rollers, run the lathe somewhat slower than you would when not using a steady. The rollers will tend to burnish their track on the workpiece. Plan to make at least a light finishing cut to clean up the track, although in many cases the burnished region can be sanded away.

A STEADY WITH A
PROJECT: CIRCULAR FRAME

This is the most common design, with three adjustable rollers to support a spindle. Make the frame from a double thickness of ¾" (19mm) MDF or plywood with two doubler pieces added near the bottom to widen the base where it sits on the ways. Use flat, ¾" (19mm) hardwood stock to make the carriers for the rollers, and add guide strips on each side of the carriers to keep them aligned.

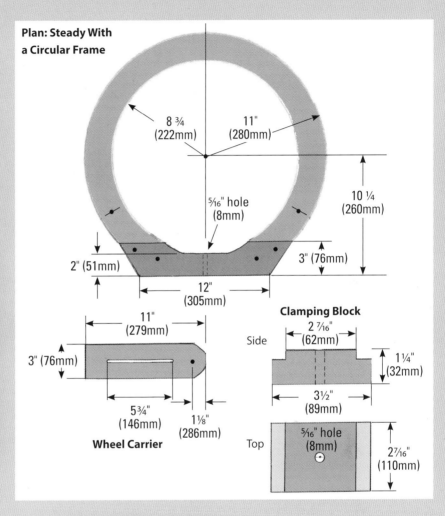

Plan: Steady With a Circular Frame

8 ¾ (222mm)
11" (280mm)
10 ¼ (260mm)
⁵⁄₁₆" hole (8mm)
2" (51mm)
3" (76mm)
12" (305mm)

Wheel Carrier

11" (279mm)
3" (76mm)
5¾" (146mm)
1⅛" (286mm)

Clamping Block

Side
2 ⁷⁄₁₆" (62mm)
1¼" (32mm)
3½" (89mm)

Top
⁵⁄₁₆" hole (8mm)
2⁷⁄₁₆" (110mm)

Step one. Cut the pieces for the frame. Use the plan as a guide to scale the frame pieces to fit your lathe. Lay out the cut lines on the stock material. Before cutting the center away, use a compass to locate six lines, equally spaced around the frame, for the bolt holes and alignment marks. Cut one piece using either a band saw or jigsaw. (You can use a band saw to make the inside cut by cutting through the base, but make the entry cut to one side of where the hole will be for the clamping bolt.) Use it as a template for the second piece. Glue the two pieces together.

Step two. Use the frame as a template for the shape of the doublers. Cut them out and drill pilot holes for screws to attach the doublers to the frame. Stand the frame upright on a flat surface. Apply wood glue to the doublers and clamp them to the frame, making sure they are pushed down against the flat surface. Screw the doublers in place.

PROJECT: A STEADY WITH A CIRCULAR FRAME *CONTINUED*

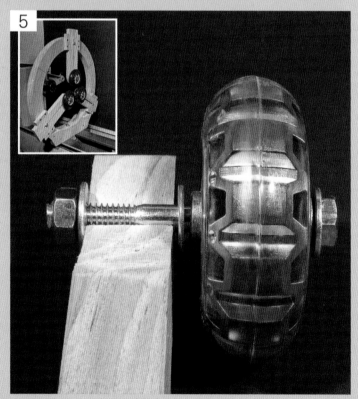

Step three. Use the plan as a guide to make a clamping block that fits the ways of your lathe. Drill a hole at the bottom center of the frame for the clamping bolt.

Step four. Make the three wheel carriers from ¾" (19mm) hardwood. Cut the pieces to size, round one end, drill the holes for the wheels, and cut the slots with a router. Drill three equally spaced holes in the frame for the bolts that hold the carriers in position. Mount the carriers on the frame, aligning them with the corresponding pencil lines on the opposite side of the frame.

Step five. Glue and screw cleats on each side of the carriers. Slip a waxed-paper shim between the carrier and the cleat to ensure that the carrier will move freely once the cleats are installed. Remove the carriers before the glue sets up so you don't inadvertently glue them in place. After the glue sets, install the wheels, using a washer on each side of the carrier, as shown in the photo at left.

A Small Spindle Steady

This is a scaled-down version of the steady shown with a circular frame, meant for spindles that are only an inch or so in diameter. Instead of skate wheels, it uses roller bearings to support the workpiece. Two versions are shown here. The first is for a lathe that has a 20" (508mm) swing. The second is for a Jet mini with a 10" (254mm) swing.

Cut the pieces for the frame. Scale the frame pieces to fit your lathe. A double thickness of ½"(13mm) plywood works well for the vertical part of the frame. As with the larger steady, glue the vertical pieces together, then screw the assembly to a ¾" (19mm) thick base that's reinforced with braces epoxied into place. Make a clamping block to fit the ways of your lathe.

Shape carriers for the roller bearings from a suitable wood. Drill three equally spaced holes in the frame for the bolts that hold the carriers in position. Attach guide strips to either side, and mount the bearings on the carriers.

Scaled down for the Jet mini, the frame of this steady is made from a single thickness of ¾" (19mm) plywood. Other details are almost identical to the one above; in fact, both use the same wheel carriers.

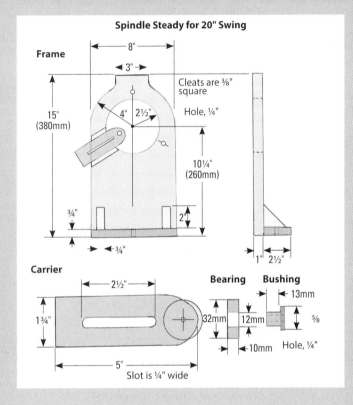

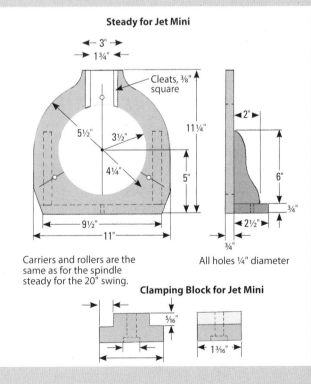

A STEADY WITH
PROJECT: VERTICAL POSTS

This steady is ideally suited for large workpieces. Two vertical threaded rods support the carriers for four scooter-wheel rollers. The rollers are fixed in the carriers but may be located at different positions to accommodate workpieces of widely differing diameters. Credit for this design goes to Herman de Vries (*www.hdv.net*), who generously granted permission for it to be included here in a slightly modified form.

Step one. Make the base and clamping block, using the plan as a guide to size the pieces to fit your lathe. Drill ¾" (19mm) diameter holes for the threaded rods and a hole for the bolt holding the clamping block. Install the threaded rods.

Step two. Make four end blocks for the wheel carriers. Drill ⅞" (22mm) holes for the threaded rods.

Step three. Cut the strips for the sides of the wheel carriers. Drill the holes for the bolts that hold the strips to the blocks. Unclamp the assembly, then locate the holes for the bolts that become the axles for the wheels. Clamp the strips together and drill holes in both pieces at the same time. Reassemble the wheel carrier with the wheels and test the fit on the base unit.

Step four. Cut the center arcs in the wheel carriers. The arcs provide clearance between the workpiece and the carriers. Locate the two holes for the axle of each wheel, making sure the holes are centered at least ½" (13mm) away from the edge of the arc. Cut the arcs, drill the holes, and assemble the steady.

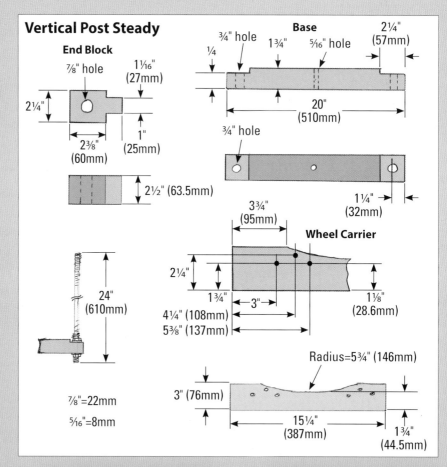

Vertical Post Steady

End Block: ⅞" hole, 1 1/16" (27mm), 2¼", 2⅜" (60mm), 1" (25mm), 2½" (63.5mm)

Base: ¾" hole, ¼, 1¾", 5/16" hole, 2¼" (57mm), 20" (510mm), ¾" hole, 1¼" (32mm)

24" (610mm)

⅞"=22mm
5/16"=8mm

Wheel Carrier: 3¾" (95mm), 2¼", 1¾", 3", 4¼" (108mm), 5⅜" (137mm), 1⅛" (28.6mm)

Radius=5¾" (146mm)

3" (76mm), 15¼" (387mm), 1¾" (44.5mm)

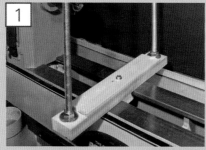

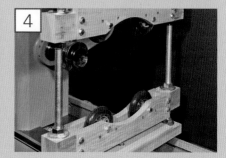

An All-Wood Steady With Vertical Posts

I made a steady with wooden vertical posts, just to see if it would work. It turned out to be surprisingly strong. What's more, you can adjust the wheel carriers quickly, without having to run several nuts up and down a threaded rod. The photos show my prototype. The arcs cut in the carriers came later.

The base is a glued-up structure of hardwood. The vertical posts are made of ½" (13mm) cabinet-grade plywood, two strips per post. The wheel carriers are ½" (13mm) plywood with rectangular hardwood blocks at the ends. They are clamped in position by 1/4-20 carriage bolts that you snug down pretty tight. I used regular nuts with fender washers instead of wing nuts or the like that are tightened by hand. I made the steady with in-line skate wheels because I had them on hand, but the larger scooter wheels will actually run more smoothly and at a lower speed.

The center member of the base is planed to a width of 1⅛" (29mm) to match the length of the axles of the wheels. The routed plywood strips that form the vertical posts are glued to the ends of the center member. Two more pieces, notched for the plywood strips, are glued to each side of this assembly. I used epoxy for its better gap-filling properties.

To build the wheel carriers, first drill the hole in each end block for the bolt that runs in the slot of the post. These holes are oversized to provide a bit of movement as the wheels are positioned against the workpiece. Install the blocks for one carrier in the posts. Drill the holes for the wheel axle bolts in the strips for the carriers and install the wheels. Fit this assembly over the end blocks and clamp it in place. Drill the holes for the bolts that hold the strips onto the end blocks. Install the bolts. Repeat this procedure for the other carrier.

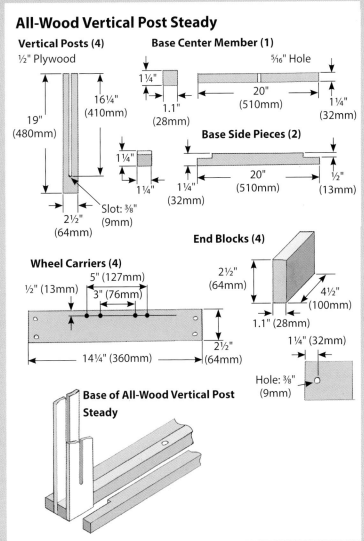

All-Wood Vertical Post Steady

Vertical Posts (4) ½" Plywood — 19" (480mm), 16¼" (410mm), 1¼", 2½" (64mm), Slot: ⅜" (9mm), 1¼"

Base Center Member (1) — 1¼", 1.1" (28mm), 20" (510mm), 1¼" (32mm), ⁵⁄₁₆" Hole

Base Side Pieces (2) — 1¼", 1¼" (32mm), 20" (510mm), ½" (13mm)

Wheel Carriers (4) — ½" (13mm), 5" (127mm), 3" (76mm), 14¼" (360mm), 2½" (64mm)

End Blocks (4) — 2½" (64mm), 4½" (100mm), 1.1" (28mm), 1¼" (32mm), Hole: ⅜" (9mm)

Base of All-Wood Vertical Post Steady

Unusual Steady. The posts of this steady are strips of plywood. The frame becomes very rigid when the wheel carriers are locked in place.

PROJECT: **A BOWL STEADY**

Sometimes, when working near the rim of a large-diameter bowl, the wall will vibrate when a tool is applied, especially if the wall is rather thin. A resonance can develop that causes a regular pattern of ripples and spirals to be produced instead of a smooth surface, and the ripples often can be removed only by extensive sanding.

The classical method for preventing the chatter is to press one hand against the outside of the bowl while making the cut. However, this is not always successful and

often produces a hot hand in addition to the chatter marks. A better way is to use a bowl steady that presses one or two wheels against the outside of the bowl.

A two-wheel version of a bowl steady is shown here. The carrier for the wheels pivots freely so the two wheels apply equal force to the bowl. The base has a slot routed down the middle so it can be moved back and forth across the ways of the lathe. An important feature of this design is a means for adjusting the force exerted on the bowl by

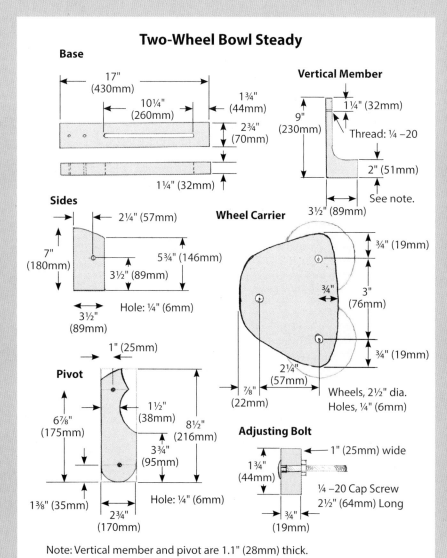

Two-Wheel Bowl Steady

Base

17" (430mm)
10¼" (260mm)
1¾" (44mm)
2¾" (70mm)
1¼" (32mm)

Vertical Member

1¼" (32mm)
9" (230mm)
Thread: ¼ –20
2" (51mm)
See note.
3½" (89mm)

Sides

2¼" (57mm)
7" (180mm)
5¾" (146mm)
3½" (89mm)
Hole: ¼" (6mm)
3½" (89mm)

Wheel Carrier

¾" (19mm)
¾"
3" (76mm)
¾" (19mm)
2¼" (57mm)
⅞" (22mm)
Wheels, 2½" dia.
Holes, ¼" (6mm)

Pivot

1" (25mm)
1½" (38mm)
8½" (216mm)
6⅞" (175mm)
3¾" (95mm)
1⅜" (35mm)
2¾" (170mm)
Hole: ¼" (6mm)

Adjusting Bolt

1" (25mm) wide
1¾" (44mm)
¼ –20 Cap Screw
2½" (64mm) Long
¾" (19mm)

Note: Vertical member and pivot are 1.1" (28mm) thick.

One- and Two-Wheelers Two types of steady rests for bowls.

Steadying. The two-wheel bowl steady in use, countering the pressure of the tools used to hollow the piece.

PROJECT: **A BOWL STEADY** *CONTINUED*

the wheels. It consists of a 1/4-20 bolt in a hole threaded through the vertical member. The end of the bolt makes contact with the pivot arm. To set up the steady, clamp the base in position so the wheels contact the bowl, then tighten the adjusting bolt to give the force you want to apply.

A one-wheel steady works at least as well as a hand applied to the outside of a bowl. I have not done a side-by-side comparison of the two versions, but I suspect the two-wheeler will give better vibration damping in difficult cases.

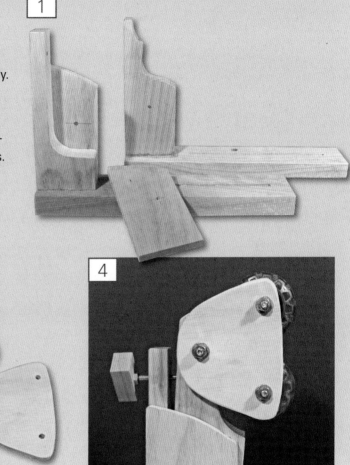

Step one. Make the base. Scale the dimensions given in the drawing to suit your lathe and applications. Rout the slot. Drill two clearance holes for the screws used to attach the vertical member, which should be planed to the same thickness as the length of the wheel axles. Shape it and attach it to the base using two long screws and a fillet of epoxy. Add the two side pieces for the two-wheel steady.

Step two. Make the pivot arm. The pivot arm for the two-wheel version is one piece and is simple to make and install. The one for the one-wheel model consists of two side pieces connected by a small block that the adjusting bolt butts against. To make it, cut out the side pieces, install the wheel, and attach the assembly to the vertical member. Then install the block that joins the two sides.

Step three. For the two-wheel model, make the carrier for the wheels. Cut out the side pieces, install the wheels, and mount the assembly on the pivot arm.

Step four. Drill and tap a hole in the vertical member for the adjusting bolt. Make a suitable knob for the bolt and install it in the hole. Shape a clamping block and drill it for a ¼" (6mm) bolt.

PROJECT: **A STRING STEADY**

Many turners enjoy the challenge of making goblets with very long stems. Other turners delight in showing off their skills by turning trembleurs (tremblers), which are long, skinny spindles with various doodads ornamenting a ridiculously long stem. These whimsical pieces are so tall and thin that they must be stabilized to keep them from flying off the lathe, but a steady with rollers cannot be used. Instead, they are constrained with a string steady like the one shown here.

String Steady. A simple plywood frame holds the string that envelops a spindle to steady it.

Step one. Make the upright part of the steady from ½" (13mm) plywood, using the plan as a guide. Glue it to a base block, reinforce the joint by gluing on triangular braces, and attach a clamping block sized to fit the ways of your lathe.

Step two. Drive four equally spaced small finish nails or small screw eyes into the upright, and glue on a small scrap block to hold the end of the string.

Step three. With the workpiece mounted on the headstock and the steady in position, install the string. You can use any fairly strong string, but watch for signs of wear. Form a small loop to hold one end of the string on a nail and wrap it as shown in the drawing. Multiple wraps are more effective. Keep the string taut at all times, and do not loop the string around the workpiece itself. To avoid having to tie a knot to keep the string taut, wrap the end around the scrap block on the upright and hold the string with a paper clamp.

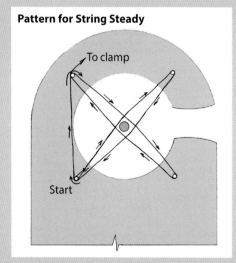

Pattern for String Steady

To clamp

Start

A TAILSTOCK-MOUNTED
PROJECT: STRING STEADY

This string steady fits into the Morse taper of the tailstock ram, a design advantage that keeps the lathe ways free. A shop-made adaptor with a Morse taper shaft holds a wood cup in position. The end of the workpiece fits into the cup and is held steady with a web of string wound around nails on the rim of the cup. Rather than make the body and the Morse taper as a single piece, I've found it preferable to turn a single Morse taper and use it as an adaptor for interchangeable cups.

Step one. To make the cup, turn a piece of spindle stock of suitable diameter between centers and form a tenon on one end. Bore a hole 1" (25mm) in diameter to a depth of about 1" (25mm) in the tenon. Reverse the piece and hollow the cup. (Rather than turn a cup, you can fabricate one as you would a vacuum drum chuck; see page 129. As the photo shows, the string is wound around nails driven into a ring that's glued to the front of the PVC drum.)

Step two. Turn the Morse taper adaptor, as explained on page 46. Turn the straight section of the adaptor to a nominal diameter of 1" (25mm). Test its fit into the hole you drilled in the cup. Carefully reduce the diameter of the adaptor until you get a tight fit.

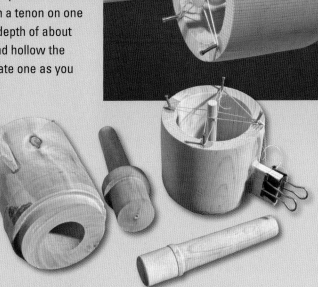

Tailstock-Mounted String Steady. The main parts of this steady are a cup to encircle the work and hold the string, plus a Morse taper adapter to fit the steady in the tailstock.

Step three. Drive four equally spaced finish nails into the rim of the cup for the string. Epoxy a scrap block onto the side of the cup to hold the free end of the string.

Step four. Mount the Morse taper adaptor and cup on the tailstock. Mount the workpiece on the lathe, with one end placed in the cup. Then hold it with a string web, formed by wrapping the string, as shown above.

PVC String Steady. An option for making a larger cup is to use a PVC pipe coupler as described for making a vacuum drum chuck. The pencil is included to give the strings something to wrap around for this photo.

A TAILSTOCK-MOUNTED PROJECT: CLOTHESPIN STEADY

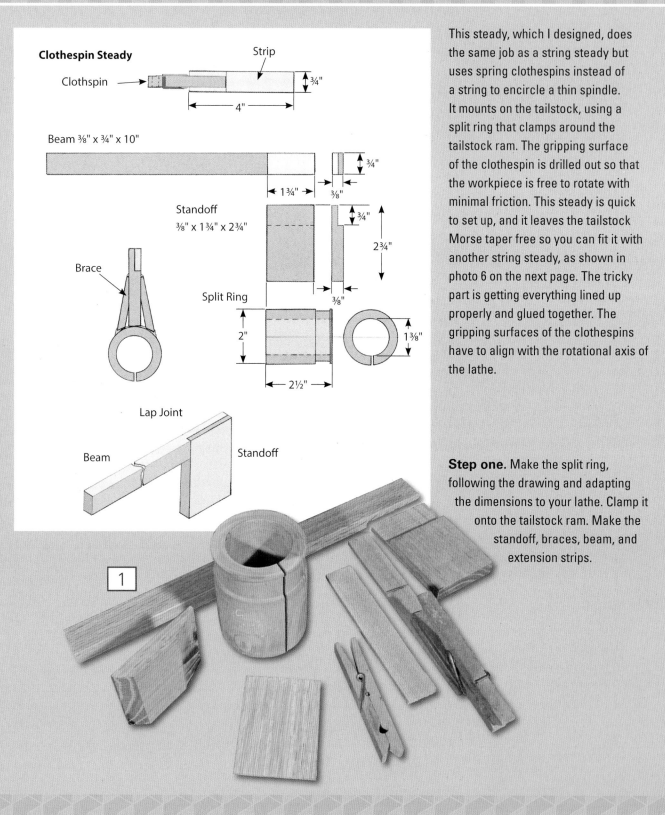

Clothespin Steady

Clothspin

Strip

¾"

4"

Beam ⅜" x ¾" x 10"

¾"

1¾"

⅜"

Standoff
⅜" x 1¾" x 2¾"

¾"

2¾"

⅜"

Brace

Split Ring

2"

1⅜"

2½"

Lap Joint

Beam

Standoff

1

This steady, which I designed, does the same job as a string steady but uses spring clothespins instead of a string to encircle a thin spindle. It mounts on the tailstock, using a split ring that clamps around the tailstock ram. The gripping surface of the clothespin is drilled out so that the workpiece is free to rotate with minimal friction. This steady is quick to set up, and it leaves the tailstock Morse taper free so you can fit it with another string steady, as shown in photo 6 on the next page. The tricky part is getting everything lined up properly and glued together. The gripping surfaces of the clothespins have to align with the rotational axis of the lathe.

Step one. Make the split ring, following the drawing and adapting the dimensions to your lathe. Clamp it onto the tailstock ram. Make the standoff, braces, beam, and extension strips.

Step two. Glue an extension strip to each clothespin. Cut a half-lap joint in the beam and standoff to attach the beam to the standoff. Glue the beam and standoff together. Mount a ⁵⁄₁₆" (8mm) dowel about 12" (305mm) long between the headstock and the tailstock ram. You may need to turn a plug to fit into the ram to hold and center the end of the dowel.

Step three. Clip a clothespin onto the dowel near the tailstock. Clamp the clothespin to the beam so that the bottom of the standoff rests flat on the split ring. Mark the clothespin strip at the top of the beam. Repeat with the other clothespin.

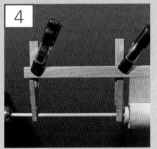

Step four. Set up the assembly. Clamp the clothespins to the beam, aligning them on the marks you made in the previous step. The bottom of the standoff should make loose contact with the split ring all along its length. Shift the bottom of the standoff forward and back (perpendicular to the axis of the lathe) until you find where it wants to be. This ensures that the gripping points of the clothespins will naturally fall on the axis of the lathe. You will probably end up with a small gap along the bottom edge of one side of the standoff, but that doesn't matter.

Step five. Tack the standoff to the split ring with medium cyanoacrylate glue to hold it in place, then add a fillet of epoxy to both sides of the standoff. Epoxy the braces to each side of the standoff. After the epoxy has set, remove the clothespins and drill out the gripping surface to the diameter you wish. If you are concerned that the clothespins may mar the surface of the work, wrap some plumber's Teflon tape around the spindle where it passes through the clothespins. If you wrap it clockwise as you look at the headstock, it will probably stay in place all by itself.

Step six. To set up the steady, clamp the split ring on the ram, clip a clothespin around the spindle to be steadied, and then bring its extension strip up to the back of the beam. Align the mark on the strip with the top of the beam, and clamp the strip in place. This photo shows three different steadies being used.

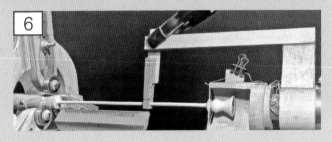

CHAPTER 11

TURNING PROJECTS

Spindle and Faceplate Exercises

This chapter shows you how to complete six popular turning projects: An endgrain box with lid, a suspended bowl with lid, a tree ornament, a ball, a classic candle holder, and a natural-edge bowl. The projects also let you practice a variety of chucking methods. It has been pointed out that I seem to be more of a technician than an artist, so feel free to modify the pieces as you see fit to improve the design. The objective is to illustrate the chucking methods, the sequence in which they are used, and to have fun.

A lid for a small box. Practice your turning skills by making a round box with a tight-fitting lid. It's one of six projects in this chapter.

A pair of cabochons.

Turners' Tape and Cabochons

A double-sided tape known as turners' tape is often useful for attaching small items to a mandrel, faceplate, or other flat surface. It has a strong adhesive and is thin enough not to be spongy. However, it is not strong enough to substitute for the screws of a faceplate or the iron grip of a scroll chuck. Let's be reasonable.

A downside of the tape is that it tends to release under a sustained pressure. For example, if you use the tape to mount a thin plate on a faceplate, it will be held securely at first but the attachment will gradually weaken under the stress of turning or sanding. It may come off the lathe.

This can be avoided if the tailstock is used to maintain a gentle pressure against the plate so the layer of tape is always under compression.

The tailstock can be removed for the hopefully brief final stages of the operation.

On the other hand, this characteristic is useful in removing a piece from the tape once the turning or sanding is done. That is, apply a steady, sustained pressure for a minute or so and it will release.

Any adhesive residue left on the workpiece can be easily removed by brushing it with lacquer thinner and then wiping with a paper towel.

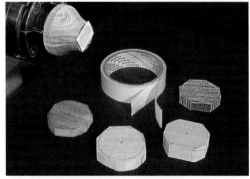

A mandrel in a chuck, tape, and blanks.

TURN A
PROJECT: CABOCHON

In traditional jewelry, a cabochon is a rounded or oval gemstone with a flat rear surface. A woodturner's version is likely to be circular and made from an interesting piece of wood. They are easy to make.

Any fine-grain hardwood that is sound can be used. For an added twist, you can use SpectraPly, GemWood, or ColorWood, which are made by laminating layers of brightly colored wood treated and held together by epoxy resin.

Step one. Install a short mandrel in your chuck and turn it to a diameter somewhat smaller than what you want the cabochon to be. Cover the face with double-sided tape.

Step two. Attach the blank for the cabochon to the tape. Use a live center with a blunt point installed in the tailstock to force the blank against the tape. *Note: If you do not have a live center with a blunt point, place a small nut or washer over the point of a cone center to keep the point from penetrating the blank.*

Step three. Turn it to a pleasing shape. Use tailstock support as much as possible during the shaping to minimize the stress on the tape.

Step four. Sand to at least 400 grit, because part of the appeal of a cabochon arises from a fine finish. Fine steel wool (0000) will bring a shine to a fine-grained hardwood.

Step five. Apply the finish of your choice. Brushing lacquer applied with a fine bristle brush works quite well. Several coats may be required to give a glossy, glass-like surface. The equivalent of a gem cutter's dop stick makes it easy to hold the cabochon during the finishing process after it is removed from the mandrel. Loctite mounting tabs provide an easy way to attach the cabochon to the dop stick (a small-diameter dowel or skewer), as shown in the photo.

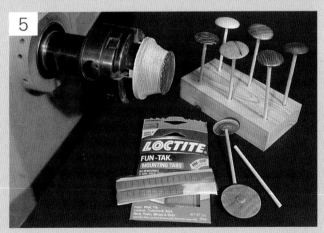

Adding a turned hole to the edge of a cabochon requires a means for mounting it off center. This can be done by replacing the simple mandrel with a carrier that, in turn, is mounted on a small screw chuck. The carrier is centered on the screw chuck for the initial turning. It is then shifted to the side for shaping the hole.

Step one. Mount the blank on the (centered) carrier and turn the cabochon.

Step two. Shift the carrier to the side. That is, attach the carrier to the screw chuck using the offset hole in the carrier.

Step three. Use a drill bit held by a Jacobs chuck in the tailstock to drill a hole through the cabochon. This is an optional step that you might find helpful.

Step four. Use a small spindle gouge to shape the area around the hole. Note that if the face of the cabochon is domed, this will be an interrupted cut. Proceed carefully and at a fairly low RPM. And that's it.

Finishing Touches

A wide variety of cords and associated hardware (findings) is available for adding the finishing touches to cabochons and pendants. The world is your oyster.

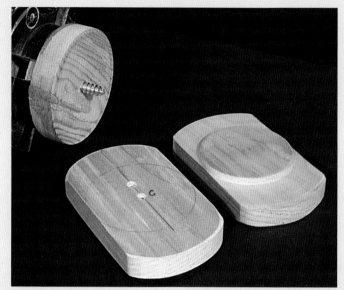
Screw chuck and two carriers.

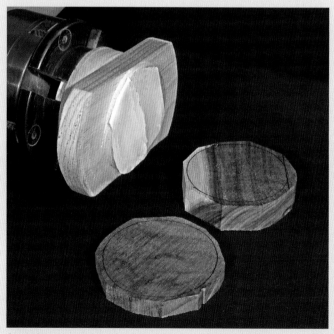
A carrier mounted on the screw chuck, with two blanks.

A pair of lathe-turned pendants.

MAKE AN ENDGRAIN
PROJECT: BOX WITH LID

It's easy to like a small box with a lid. There are many different types and styles you can make. Here are the basic steps for making one type of small turned box. A flange on the lid fits over a lip on the base to join the parts. You use a scroll chuck for most of the work, but you also use the base as a jam chuck for the lid, and you make a second jam chuck so you can finish the base.

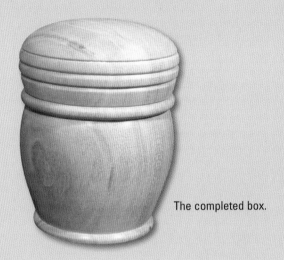

The completed box.

Step one. Begin with a blank that you can turn to a cylinder between 2" and 3" (51 and 76mm) in diameter. The blank should be about 2" (51mm) greater than the height of the finished box, but the exact length depends somewhat on the design. Mount the blank between centers and turn it to a cylinder. Form tenons on both ends. Mark a line on the blank where you will part it into two pieces, one for the base and the other for the lid. Begin the cut with a parting tool and finish with a small saw with the lathe stationary.

Step two. Install the tenon on the top part in a scroll chuck. True the outside and square up the exposed face. At this time, decide upon the diameter for the inside of the lid flange and mark it on the end of the blank. Hollow the inside of the lid. Gradually work close to the line marking the flange, then use a scraper to define its inside surface. Be sure the sides of the flange are parallel, not dovetailed or tapered. Turn the outside profile of the top, going as far toward the center of the blank as you can. Finally, make a light pass with a scraper to be sure the flange is still true. Then part off the top.

Step three. Mount the base section in a scroll chuck and true it up. Square up the exposed face. Transfer the inner diameter of the flange in the top to the face of the base. Make another circle to represent the inside diameter of the lip on the base. Mark the length of the base lip on the outside. Turn the outside profile to very nearly its final shape. Use a skew to incise a sharp line at the bottom of the lip. Form the lip, leaving it slightly oversize. Hollow the inside of the base; this goes faster if you bore a hole to establish the depth of the hollow.

Step four. Begin fitting the lid by turning a shallow taper on the lip on the base so the lid will just begin to fit over it. With the lathe off, press the lid over the lip and turn the spindle by hand to burnish a fine line where the two parts make contact. This will mark the diameter to which the flange should be turned. Gradually reduce the diameter of the lip on the base to the size indicated by the burnish mark. Proceed slowly and test the fit often. Aim for a tight, press-on fit because you will use the base as a jam chuck to finish turning the top of the lid.

Step five. Press the lid onto the base. Bring the tailstock up for support and finish the outside profile of the lid, paying attention to the join line between the base and the lid. As you work toward the top of the lid, pull the tailstock back so the entire top of the lid is accessible. If you deem it advisable, you can tape the lid to the base to give an added measure of support. Complete the top of the lid, then remove it from the base. Fine-tune the fit of the lid by scraping a small amount of wood from the lip on the base. Do not use sandpaper because sanding will likely cause the lip to go out of round and make a good fit hard to achieve.

Step six. Part off the base, using a parting tool and a saw. Turn a jam chuck to fit the opening in the base. Reverse-chuck the base onto the jam chuck, using the tailstock to support the work, and clean up the bottom. If the fit of the base on the jam chuck is tight, you may be able to remove the tailstock and make the final cuts with the base still on the lathe. Otherwise, turn the bottom down to a nubbin and finish it off the lathe.

MAKE A
PROJECT: ROLLING PIN

A traditional rolling pin.

Three types of these functional items are commonly encountered: the traditional with integrated (non-rotating) handles, the traditional with rotating handles, and the French style with gently tapered ends instead of handles.

A rolling pin with non-rotating handles is basically a spindle and is easy to turn. But if the handles must rotate independently of the body, the process is a bit more involved. One method for making the rotating handles is described in the following. It involves making the body, two bushings, and two handles. The handles are attached with two ¼"-20 hex bolts (or metric M6 x 1) as shown in the diagram above right.

The dimensions can be customized to your liking. For a traditional body, the diameter ranges from 1 ¾" to 2.375" (44.5 to 60.3mm), with the length ranging from about 10" to 13" (254 to 330.2mm).

Step one. Select a blank about ¾" (19mm) longer than the desired finished length of the body. Mount the blank between centers and form a tenon on each end.

Step two. Remount the blank in a scroll chuck using a center on the tailstock to accurately align the blank. Install a Jacobs chuck on the tailstock and then use a ¾" (19mm) twist drill bit to drill a hole 2.375" (50mm) deep into the end of the body, measured from the face of the tenon. Repeat for the other end.

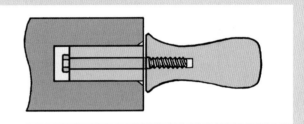

Body, bushings, and handle as viewed from the side.

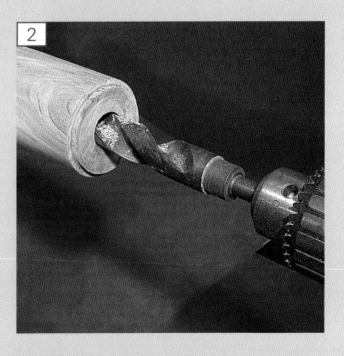

Step three. Install the blank between a mandrel at the headstock and a cone center on the tailstock. Turn the blank to its final diameter and then sand to the final finish.

Step four. Remove the tenon from each end of the blank and sand the ends as necessary. This completes the body.

Step five. To turn the bushings, begin with a dowel rod or turn a spindle to a diameter of at least ⅞" (22mm). Cut two sections 1 ½" (38mm) long from this blank. Using the lathe or a drill press, drill a ¼" (6mm) hole through each section.

Step six. Mount one of the sections between a mandrel and a cone center and turn it to a uniform diameter to match the holes in the body. Provide for a loose, sliding fit. Repeat for the remaining section. This completes the bushings.

Step seven. For handles 3" (76mm) long, place a blank 6¾" (170mm) long between centers and turn it to a uniform diameter somewhat greater than 1" (25mm). Turn a groove ¾" (19mm) wide and ⅛" (3mm) deep at the center of the blank.

Step eight. Use a parting tool to separate the blank into two parts. Make the cut in the middle of the groove so that each half has a tenon on the end.

Step nine. Mount one of the sections in a scroll chuck and drill a hole into the end at least 1 ⅛" (28mm) deep. Make the diameter of this hole such that the handle can be screwed onto the bolt that passes through the bushing. For a ¼"-20 bolt, a diameter of 0.228" works well. This is the diameter of a #1 bit from a set of number drill bits. If you're working in the metric system, use a comparable bolt and corresponding drill bit. If your chuck will not grip a spindle as small as 1" (25mm) diameter, use a hand drill or a drill press to drill the hole.

When making multiple rolling pins, it is worth the effort to make a threaded mandrel for mounting the blank. This allows the handle to be finished to completion on the lathe. Otherwise, mount it between an unthreaded mandrel and a cone center.

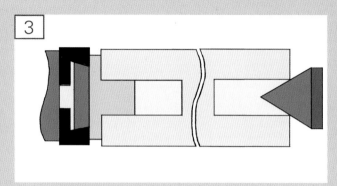

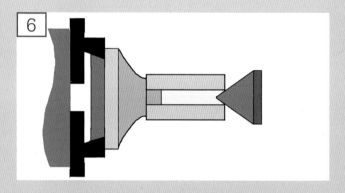

Step ten. Screw one of the blanks onto the threaded mandrel and use a cone center on the tailstock for additional support. Turn the handle to the desired profile. Remove the tailstock support for the last bit of turning. Sand to the desired finish. Repeat. This completes the handles.

Step eleven. Apply a bit of wax to the shaft of a bolt and the threaded end of a handle. Then, insert the bolt through one of the bushings. Screw the handle onto the bolt. Leave about ¹⁄₁₆" (2mm) space between the bushing and handle.

Step twelve. Apply a small amount of epoxy to the surface of the bushing and then push the bushing into the body. Ensure that excess epoxy does not get pushed up between the body and the handle. Check the handle for free rotation as the epoxy cures. Repeat.

Step thirteen. Apply a finish. The ideal finish is a mixture of mineral oil and beeswax. However, any food-safe oil that does not go rancid will work just fine.

A French rolling pin.

French Rolling Pin

A French rolling pin is basically a spindle with tapered ends and is therefore easy to turn. Just mount a blank between centers and let the fun begin. We can, however, make the project more interesting by having the ends (handle parts) made of a contrasting wood. That is what is described here.

There are two methods for attaching the ends to the main body. One is to join the parts using a short dowel for reinforcement at the interface. The other, illustrated here, is to turn a short tenon on each handle and then insert the tenon into a hole in the body.

The diameter of a French roller is typically about 1¾" (45mm) and has an overall length of about 20" (500mm). The handle sections may range from about 3" (76mm) to 4 ½" (115mm). This means the length of the body will range from about 11" to 14" (280 mm to 355mm), depending upon your design.

Step one. Mount the blank for the body between centers and turn a tenon (for the scroll chuck) on each end. Keep the diameter of the two tenons greater than 1 ¾" (45mm), the finished diameter of the body. Square the ends of the blank.

Step two. Install the blank in a scroll chuck. Drill a ⅝" (16mm) hole about 1" (25mm) deep into the end. Reverse the blank and repeat. The blanks for the handle sections need to be about 2" (50mm) longer than the finished length of the handles to allow for the tenon and to give room for parting off the completed rolling pin.

Step three. Mount a blank for one of the handles between centers. Form a tenon (for the scroll chuck) on the end of the blank that will be near the end of the completed rolling pin.

Remove the blank from between centers and then install it between a scroll chuck and a point center on the tailstock.

Step four. Turn the tenon that will be used to join the handle to the body. Make it about ¾" (19mm) long and ⅝" (16mm) diameter. Test the diameter as you go and be sure to get a good fit where the handle joins the body. Repeat for the other blank.

Step five. Attach the handle blanks to the body with epoxy. Jam the glued-up blank between the headstock and tailstock to apply clamping pressure while the epoxy cures.

At this point, we have a three-section blank with a tenon on each end and with the end centers marked. Only a bit of routine spindle turning remains to be done, and after the finish is applied, it will be ready to use.

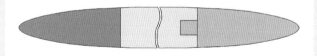

The handle is attached to the body by a tenon on the handle.

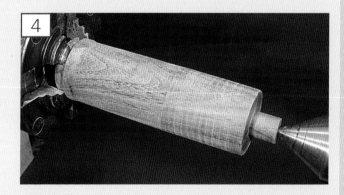

Stand for Rolling Pin

This stand consists of a base, a platform, and two spindles. The base should be about 6" (150mm) in diameter and ideally about 1" (25mm) thick. The spindles are turned from blanks 5¼" (135mm) long overall including the tenons.

Making the base and spindles only involves straightforward turning techniques. The platform, however, is more demanding. How to make it is described in the following. Begin with a rectangular blank 7" (180mm) long that is ¾" (19mm) thick and wide enough to accommodate the rolling pin.

If you don't have flat woodworking equipment to bring the blank to the proper thickness, screw it to a backing plate (as described below) and use turning tools to do it. Be sure to sink the screw heads well below the surface, for obvious reasons.

Traditional rolling pin with stand.

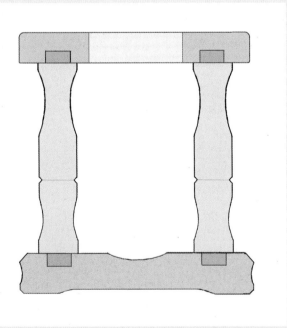

Step one. Draw the plan view of the platform on the lower side of the blank. Make the hole diameter about ⅛" (3mm) larger than the rolling pin intended for the stand. Mark the center of the hole. Use a drill press to drill a ¼" (6mm) hole through the center.

Step two. Mount the blank on a backing plate using two wood screws. Use the center hole and a cone center to position the blank on the backing plate. Turn and shape one side of the hole, but do not cut the hole all the way through.

Step three. Reverse the blank on the backing plate, again using the center hole to position the blank. (You cannot use the same screw holes in the backing plate.) Finish turning and shaping the hole.

Step four. Use a drill press and a Forstner bit to drill the ⅝" (16mm) holes for the tenons on the spindles. Make the holes about ⅜" (9.5mm) deep.

Step five. Use a band saw to cut out the platform from the rectangular blank. Sand the outer edge smooth and round the sharp corners. Apply a finish to all components.

Step six. Assemble the stand using epoxy to hold the spindles in place.

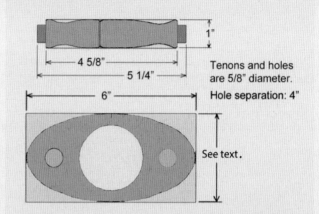

4 5/8"
5 1/4"
1"
6"
Tenons and holes are 5/8" diameter.
Hole separation: 4"
See text.

3

MAKE A SUSPENDED
PROJECT: BOWL WITH LID

A suspended bowl—one with four "wings" supporting the bowl itself—is an eye-catching piece. It is relatively easy to make, with a bit of precise tool handling. But it is also easy to destroy if you slip up while turning the wings. You can leave the bowl open, add a top, or add a top adorned with a knob or finial.

Suspended bowls with lids.

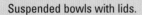

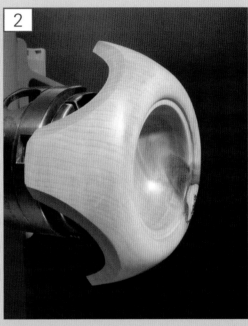

Step one. Begin by mounting a square blank of sound wood on a screw chuck. Orient the blank so that the side to be the bottom faces the tailstock. Place the tool rest near the blank, perpendicular to the lathe axis. This will protect your fingers from the whirling wings, which become almost invisible when the piece spins. Form the contour of the wings and the underside of the bowl. Form a tenon on the bottom of the bowl and mark its center.

Step two. Remove the piece from the screw chuck and install it in a scroll chuck, using the tenon you just made. Shape the top surface of the wings. If necessary, reattach the piece to the screw chuck to modify the profile of the wings. That done, mount the piece in the scroll chuck again and hollow the interior of the bowl. If the bowl will have a lid, decide how the lid will seat on the bowl. Cut any necessary shoulders or flat surfaces.

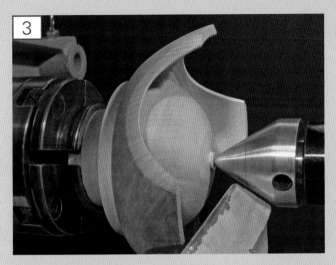

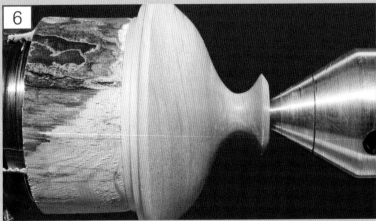

Step three. Turn a fixture to jam chuck the workpiece. Reverse-chuck the bowl, again keeping the tool rest perpendicular to the lathe axis to protect your fingers. Reduce the tenon on the bottom to a small nubbin. Finish it off the lathe.

Step four. Mount a new blank on a screw chuck, true it up, and shape the top. Leave room to form a tenon. You may want to add a finial or knob to the lid, so prepare the seat for it now. To do that, turn the blank to the lid's exact height and clean up the area where the finial is to be attached. Drill a hole to form a shallow recess to hold a tenon on the bottom of the finial. Then form a tenon in the wood surrounding the recess.

Step five. Reverse the blank and mount it in a scroll chuck, using the tenon on the top. Begin hollowing the interior, then refine the rim so that it matches the seating surface on the bowl. Complete the interior and add whatever decorative elements you want to the underside.

Step six. Jam chuck the lid against a flat surface. Bring up the point of a cone center to make contact with the bottom of the recess for the finial. Remove the tenon around the recess and finish shaping the top profile. Add a knob or finial.

MAKE A GLOBE-TYPE
PROJECT: TREE ORNAMENT

Ornaments make delightful gifts. Turning them allows you to practice hollowing small forms through a relatively small opening, and turning the icicle lets you hone your spindle-turning skills. And if coloring wood is your thing, ornaments provide abundant opportunities for showing off your talents.

A diameter of about 2" (51mm) for the globe is a good starting point, with an icicle about 3" (76mm) long. The finial (top part) should be about 1" (25mm) tall. Once you have made several, you will get a feel for what seems best.

Globe-type tree ornament.

Step one. Mount a spindle blank between centers and rough it to a cylinder with a tenon at one end. Mount the workpiece in a scroll chuck using the tenon. Shape the outside of the globe. Leave enough wood next to the chuck to support the globe when you hollow it.

Step two. Drill a ⅝" (16mm) diameter hole in the globe so that it ends about ¼" (6mm) from the bottom. Measure carefully; wrap a piece of tape on the bit to mark the depth. Hollow the globe, making the wall as thin as you dare. Leave enough wood to support the icicle and the finial where they attach. Flatter globes need more material in these areas because of the end grain. Use the hole you drilled as a depth indicator when working near the bottom. After the hollowing is complete, finish the outside profile and sand the globe.

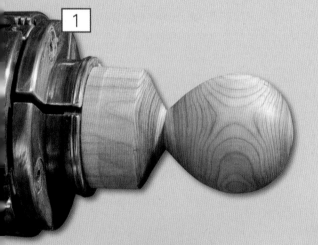

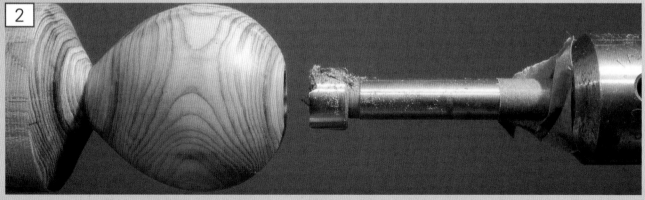

Step three. To free the globe, turn the end at the headstock down to a diameter slightly less than ½" (13mm). With a ½" (13mm) Forstner bit in a Jacobs chuck in the tailstock, continue the hole that was drilled earlier. As the bit cuts through, the globe will break away and come to rest on the shaft of the bit.

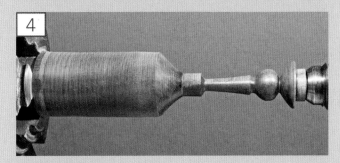

Step four. The icicle is simply a finial that hangs downward. Follow the steps on page 20 to turn a finial with a tenon at one end. The tenon should be about ½" (13mm) in diameter, but test the fit when you get close to the final diameter. Undercut the shoulder of the tenon a small amount for a smooth seam where the finial meets the globe.

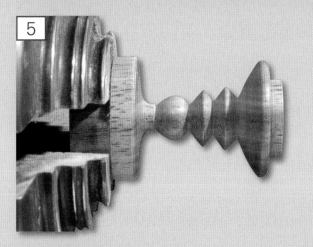

Step five. Shape the finial; this is the shorter, top section of the ornament that includes a way to hang the ornament. Mount a short spindle blank about 1" (25mm) in diameter and 2" (51mm) long in a scroll chuck. At the tailstock end, form a short tenon that will be used to attach the finial to the globe. It should be about ⅝" (16mm) in diameter. Check the fit to be sure, and undercut the base slightly so it will fit nicely on the globe. Shape the body, beginning with the area near the base. Roughly shape the region where the hanger will be, and then part it off.

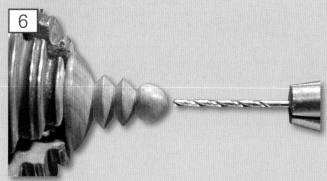

Step six. Reverse-chuck the finial, using the tenon at the base to hold the piece in the scroll chuck. Refine the top as necessary. Use the point of the live center to make a small dimple in the center. Mount a small drill bit in a Jacobs chuck and drill a hole for the hanger, using the dimple to center the drill bit. Drill a small pilot hole if you plan to use a screw eye as the hanger. If you intend to use a wire to make your own hanger, drill the hole all the way through. Dress the end with fine sandpaper. Apply your finish of choice, install the hanger, and glue the three pieces together using medium cyanoacrylate or epoxy.

PROJECT: **TURN A BALL**

There is something appealing and captivating about a perfectly round wooden ball that shows no marks from the lathe. A ball may not be the most useful item, but making one tests your skills. When the outcome is good, turning a ball can be rather gratifying to a lonely turner.

A collection of turned balls.

Step one. Mount a blank between centers that is about 2" (51mm) longer than its thickness. Turn it to a uniform cylinder and measure the diameter. Mark the midpoint of the cylinder. Make two more marks on either side that are a distance from the midpoint equal to the radius of the cylinder. These marks define the ends of the ball. Mark two more lines half the radius from the midpoint, and finally, mark two additional lines three-fourths the radius from the midpoint.

Step two. Use a thin parting tool to make defining cuts part-way through the cylinder at these lines. Make the cuts on the side of the line away from the midpoint. Part of the line should still be visible when you finish the cut. For the lines one-half the radius from the midpoint, cut to a depth equal to one-eighth the radius. For the lines three-fourths the radius from the midpoint, cut to a depth equal to one-third the radius. The depth is not critical at the outer lines; one-half the radius is a good place to start.

Step three. Begin shaping the ball, using the benchmark cuts as a rough guide. If you wish, make a template and use it to check the curve. When you are satisfied with the shape, cut away the waste at the ends to leave two small nubbins holding the ball. Remove the ball from the lathe and cut away the nubbins.

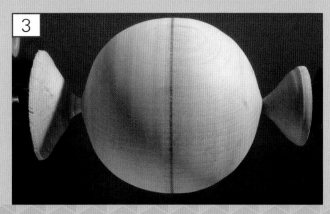

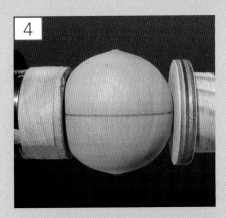

Step four. Refine the shape of the ball. Mount the ball between a cup center at the headstock and a flat fixture on the tailstock live center with the rotational axis of the ball at right angles to what it was before. Be sure the ball is seated properly. Apply pressure with the tailstock to hold everything together.

Step five. Start the lathe and look across the top of the rotating ball. Unless your ball is already perfectly round, you will see a ghost. This refers to the narrow region right at the edge of the ball where the surface doesn't appear to be solid. Imagine a football rotating rapidly end over end. Your objective is to turn away the ghost. Avoid removing any wood at the bottom of the ghost where it meets the solid-looking surface. What you are doing is removing the ends of the football.

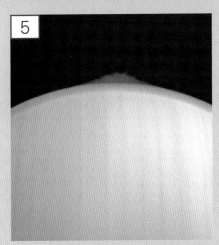

Step six. Once the ghost is gone, loosen the fixtures and shift the rotational axis about 60 degrees to one side or the other. Retighten the fixtures and repeat the process of removing the ghost. Chances are that you will need to take only very fine cuts. Loosen the fixtures and shift the rotational axis 120 degrees in the opposite direction. Tighten everything down and start the lathe. At this point, you should see only a very small ghost. If it is not small, maybe even larger than before, either you are not seating the ball in the fixtures properly or you are cutting too deeply and into the bottom of the ghost.

Step seven. After you are satisfied with the way you have removed the ghost (and it doesn't have to be perfect) use the fixtures to hold the ball while you sand it. At left front in the photo is a small cup center that can be used in lieu of the flat fixture. It fits over the live center. When the sanding is done, admire your work. Roll the ball across a flat tabletop. Does it roll in a straight line?

PROJECT: MAKE A HOLDER FOR CANDLES OR CONFETTI LIGHTS

A classic candleholder is relatively easy to make. If you wish, you can size it to hold a confetti light (a small oil reservoir with a wick) instead of a real candle. The holder consists of three parts, a base, a cup, and a finger ring to make it portable. Making the candleholder entails five different chucking methods, plus a special method for sanding the ring and a custom jig to mount the ring on the base.

Classic candleholder.

Step one. Begin with the base. Use a screw chuck to hold a circular blank at least 1¼" (32mm) thick and large enough to yield a base 6" (152mm) in diameter. True up the edge, then shape the bottom profile. Flatten an area at the center of the bottom so you can glue a waste block there. Turn the waste block and size it to fit your scroll chuck.

Step two. Remove the piece from the screw chuck, turn it around, and use a scroll chuck to grip the waste block. Shape the top surface. At the rim, turn a contour that matches the outer diameter of the finger ring. Shape the pedestal in the center and cut a seating surface for the cup. Drill a ⅝"-diameter (16mm) hole to accept a tenon that will be formed on the bottom of the cup. Reverse-chuck the piece (inset) to remove the waste block and complete the bottom.

Step three. Cut a suitable blank for the cup. Make it about 4" (102mm) long. If it will hold a regular candle, figure on a minimum diameter of 1½" (38mm); for a confetti light, a minimum diameter of 2¼" (57mm). Mount the blank between centers, true it up, and form a tenon on one end for a scroll chuck. Then mount the blank in the chuck and clean up the exposed end.

Step four. Hollow the cup for the type of light you plan to use. A confetti light is about 1½" (38mm) in diameter and flat on the bottom. The bottom of a candle has a ⅞"-long (22mm) taper, which is about ⅞" (22mm) in diameter at the top and ¾" (19mm) at the bottom. Candles vary considerably, however, so try to have a candle at hand for test fits. Rough out the socket for the candle with a ¾" (19mm) Forstner bit, drilling ⅞" (22mm) deep. Use a spindle gouge or small scraper to form the taper.

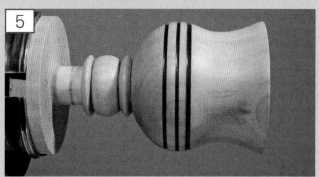

Step five. Turn the outside profile. Bring your artistic abilities forward. Cut a square shoulder at the bottom of the stem and form the tenon to match the hole in the top of the pedestal. Part off the piece at the end of the tenon.

Step six. Make the ring from copper plumbing pipe with a 1" (25mm) inside diameter. Shape a one-ended mandrel to hold the ring. Finish the edges of the ring with a sharp file. Then run the lathe at slow speed and sand the ring. Begin with 320 grit and see if all scratches are removed. Work through the grits, ending with 600 grit. Fine steel wool (0000) will give the copper a nice shine.

Step seven. Make a fixture to aid in sanding the inside of the ring. Install a ⅝" (16mm) dowel about 3½" (89mm) long in a scroll chuck. Cut a strip of 150-grit sandpaper about 3" (76mm) long and about 2½" (64mm) wide. Wrap this around the dowel in a direction so that the spinning dowel will tighten the wrap. Then tape the sandpaper closest to the chuck. Take a strip of 320-grit paper about 5" (13cm) long and 1¾" (44mm) wide and stick the end of it under the flap of the 150-grit paper. Wrap the 320-grit strip around the 150-grit paper. Slip the ring over the sandpaper and start the lathe.

Step eight. Make a jig to hold the base and the ring steady as you epoxy the ring in place, using the photo at left as a guide. Use coarse sandpaper or the burr of a rotary tool to rough up the surface of the ring where it will contact the rim.

Step nine. Clamp the base in place. Slip the ring over the dowel on the jig, and place the ring where it is to go on the rim. Clamp the strip holding the ring. Lift the ring far enough to apply epoxy to the seat for the ring, then lower the ring into the epoxy and be sure it is seated properly. Once this epoxy has cured, remove the piece from the jig and apply more epoxy to form a tiny fillet around the ring. Attach the cup to the base.

TURN A
PROJECT: NATURAL-EDGE BOWL

To a casual viewer, this bowl appears more elliptical than round, which may have some admirers asking how you turned the piece.

One of the challenges in turning a natural-edge bowl is keeping the bark intact. Your chances are better for keeping the bark if the tree (or blank) is cut in midwinter, when the sap is down. If it's cut when the sap is up, the bark is almost certain to come off the piece. Thin cyanoacrylate wicked into the region where the bark joins the wood will improve the odds for keeping it, but this is not a sure-fire fix. In any event, keeping the bark is an option, not a requirement.

The procedure given below begins with mounting the blank on a faceplate, which is the safest method for your first natural-edge piece. As you gain experience, you may skip the faceplate and go directly to step three, where the blank is mounted between centers. This will avoid any issues that may arise with the holes made by the faceplate screws.

Natural-edge wooden bowl.

Step one. Begin with a length of timber, such as a large tree limb. Use a band saw or chain saw to cut a flat on one side of the blank. Mount it on a faceplate and install it on the lathe. The blank shown in the photo is a limb from an ornamental plum tree. The off-center pith made it an excellent choice for a natural-edge bowl.

Step two. Use the tailstock for additional support and rough out the outside profile. Make the initial cuts toward hollowing the bowl, aiming to remove the bark at the center. Turn or drill a recess in the bottom to form a seat for a drive center. Pull the tailstock back as needed to do the turning near the center.

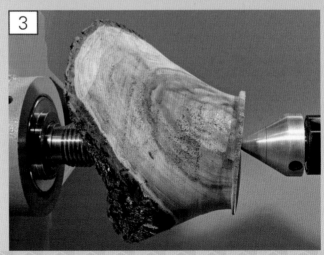

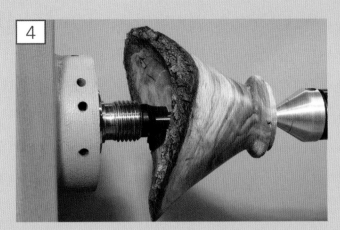

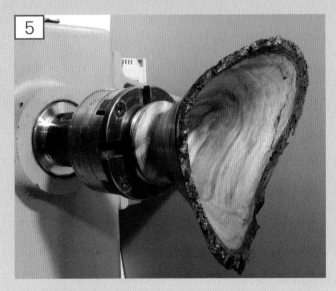

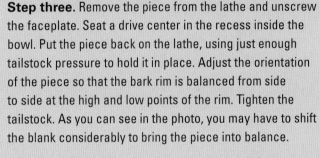

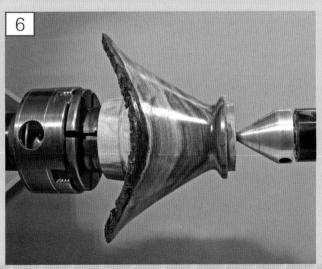

Step three. Remove the piece from the lathe and unscrew the faceplate. Seat a drive center in the recess inside the bowl. Put the piece back on the lathe, using just enough tailstock pressure to hold it in place. Adjust the orientation of the piece so that the bark rim is balanced from side to side at the high and low points of the rim. Tighten the tailstock. As you can see in the photo, you may have to shift the blank considerably to bring the piece into balance.

Step four. True the outside, square the end, and form a tenon near the tailstock. Turn the outside profile to its final shape and sand the surface with the lathe turned off, using a sanding pad mounted in a drill. Do not try to sand the piece with the lathe running because of the hazard presented by the rotating wings and because the leading edge of the wings will invariably be rounded off. Apply a coat of lacquer sanding sealer to the outside to help keep the bark on the rim.

Step five. Mount the piece in a scroll chuck, using the tenon you formed on the base. Position the tool rest perpendicular to the lathe axis to protect your hands from the whirling rim, and finish hollowing the interior. Aim for a uniform thickness so the width of the rim will be very nearly the same all the way around the bowl.

Step six. Reverse-chuck the piece, holding it on an internal jam chuck with the tailstock. Finish turning the foot. Remove most of the tenon and refine the shape of the foot. With the bowl off the lathe, remove the nubbin at the center of the foot and apply your finish of choice.

CHAPTER 12

ASSEMBLED PIECES

Bowls and Vessels Made in Several Parts

One way to make a bowl or platter more interesting and attractive is to add a foot or rim of contrasting wood. Adding a foot is easy. Adding a rim is a bit more complicated, but I'll show you a simple trick that you can use with some precise turning for good results almost every time.

Bowls and vessels don't have to be made from a single piece. You can build up a finial or a pedestal by joining small elements This lets you incorporate contrasting woods as well as minimize waste when working with expensive wood. I'll explain in detail how to make small parts that fit together to form a finished piece.

Finally, I'll show you two tricks for making hollow forms. One, how to make a hollow form with a small opening—but without working through the opening. You cut the vessel into two parts, hollow each one individually, and reassemble the parts. If you're clever, you can hide the joint so the piece looks as if it were hollowed from the top. Two, how to hollow a tall vessel through the bottom, then plug the hole to mask where you did the hollowing.

Half a hollow form. This chapter shows how to assemble handsome turned objects from several parts. Here, the bottom half of a vessel is being finished and will be attached to its mate.

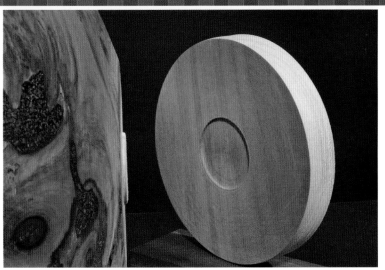

Ready. The bottom of a bowl prepared to receive a foot.

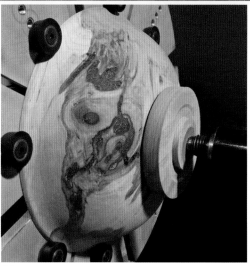

Glue-Up. Use the tailstock to apply pressure to the new foot while the glue sets.

How to Attach a Foot to a Bowl

A foot is decorative, of course, but it serves other purposes, too. It adds thickness to the bottom of a bowl to cover a defect in the wood or to mask the fact that you turned the bowl too deeply. You can even use a foot to cover wood so degraded that it will not cut cleanly or withstand the grip of the chuck jaws.

Begin by preparing the bottom of the bowl. You may want to turn a stubby tenon or shallow recess to center the foot; be sure the area surrounding the tenon or recess is dead flat. However, if you use the point center of the tailstock to center the blank for the new foot, you can skip the tenon or recess. Just be sure the bottom is flat so the foot joins securely with a minimal glue line.

It is easiest to add the foot in the course of shaping the outside, with the workpiece still mounted on a faceplate or screw chuck. But you may find it easier to add the foot after you have shaped the outside and hollowed

the bowl. This approach requires a method for reverse-chucking the piece without tailstock support, such as by using Cole jaws, a Longworth chuck, or a vacuum chuck. You can use the tailstock and normal jam-chucking, but this requires working around the point of the live center.

Select a blank for the new foot somewhat larger than what the final foot will be. True it up and form a tenon or add a waste block and mount the disk in a scroll chuck. Cut a tenon or recess to match what you formed on the base of the vessel. Be sure the new foot seats properly, with no gap at the join line. Glue the foot in place; use the tailstock to clamp it while the glue dries.

Once the glue has cured, shape the foot's profile and blend it in with the side of the vessel. If necessary, add decorative beads or grooves to hide any gaps or ragged edges that may appear at the glue line.

How to Add a Decorative Rim to a Bowl

Here's the basic procedure: Prepare the rim to receive the ring, true a disk from which the ring will be cut, and match the glue surfaces of the ring and the rim. Then glue the disk to the rim, remove the interior of the disk, and shape the ring. The details of the procedure differ, depending on whether the wall of the bowl is very nearly vertical near the rim, or whether it slopes inward or outward. The tricky part is getting a good fit between the rim and the ring at the glue line.

That's easy if the wall of the bowl is nearly vertical. The ring's seat can be perpendicular to the axis of the lathe and flattened with a sanding block. You glue the disk to the rim, remove the center of the disk, and blend the remaining ring to the shape of the bowl.

But if the bowl wall flares out or turns in too much, you will need to shape the rim and the ring to keep the angle between the glue line and the outside close to 90 degrees. If the angle is overly acute, you will get sharp, feathered edges on the ring and bowl, which can tear out.

You can make a simple but effective angle gauge from a strip of wood and a finish nail. Hold the strip across the rim of the bowl and mark an angle across it that matches the angle on the bowl. Drill a hole through the strip that matches the angle, and then insert a finishing nail through the hole. Be sure you can push the nail back and forth.

Credit for the angle gauge goes to Earl Kennedy of the Piedmont-Triad Woodturners Association in Greensboro, North Carolina.

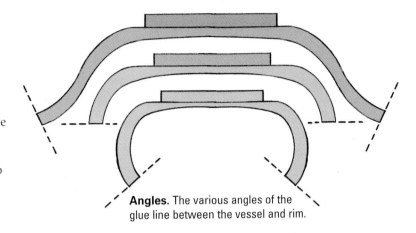

Angles. The various angles of the glue line between the vessel and rim.

Angle-Gauge Setup. To make a simple angle gauge, mark the angle of the glue surface of the bowl on the strip used for the angle gauge, then install a nail at that same angle.

For a Bowl With a Vertical Rim

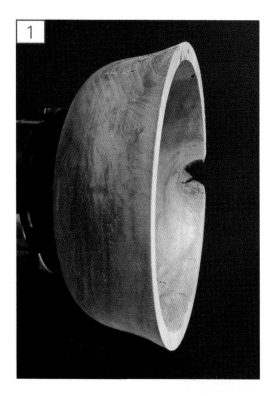

Step one. With the foot of the bowl held by a scroll chuck, flatten the rim with turning tools and a sanding block.

Step two. Mount a blank for the decorative rim on the lathe and flatten it in the area where it will join the bowl. Glue the blank for the decorative rim to the bowl.

Step three. Once the glue has set, use a parting tool to remove the center portion of the disk. Shape the rim so it blends with the contours of the bowl.

For a Bowl With an Inward-Sloping Rim

The opening in the bowl and the outside of the decorative rim are tapered so that the ring fits the opening like a cork in a bottle.

Step one. Locate the point on the bowl where the ring is to be applied and determine the angle for the mating surfaces. Make the cut that defines the angle on the bowl, but leave a bit of room for small adjustments. Make the angle gauge. Adjust the angle of the bowl rim to match that of the nail through the strip. Hold a small flashlight underneath the nail to see the gap between the nail and the rim.

Step two. Keep the bowl mounted in the chuck and remove the assembly from the lathe. Mount the disk for the decorative rim on a screw chuck. Turn it close to its final diameter. Cut the mating angle on the blank, checking it with the angle gauge. (The inset shows how accurate the angle gauge can be.) Adjust the overall diameter of the blank so that it will contact the rim near the midpoint of its thickness. (The blue sphere on the live center is the interior of a golf ball, made by Earl Kennedy.)

Step three. When you are satisfied with the rim angle, remove it from the lathe. Remount the bowl and glue the disk to the rim. When the glue has set, turn away the central portion of the disk. Refine the shape of the ring, as shown in the photo at bottom right; hollowing tools may be required for the inner surface.

For a Bowl With an Outward-Sloping Rim

The glue surface on the ring must be formed on its inside diameter. Once you have trued up the disk for the ring, part off the section for the ring and mount it in Cole jaws or on a backing plate to cut the angle.

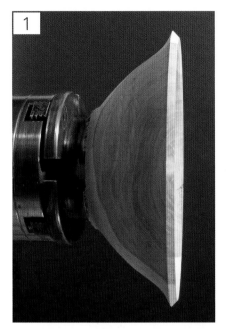

Step one. Prepare the rim of the bowl to optimize the glue angle. Remove the assembly from the lathe.

Step two. Mount the disk, using a screw chuck or waste block to true it. Part off the ring, leaving plenty of wood on the inside. Mount it in Cole jaws or on a backing plate using holddowns. Orient the ring so the glue surface faces the tailstock. If you use Cole jaws, tack spacers to the ring with a drop of cyanoacrylate to make the ring stand away from the jaws. Slip spacers under the ring if you use a backing plate.

Step three. Form the glue angle on the inside of the ring. Apply glue to the mating surfaces and use the tailstock to press the bowl against the ring. If you used spacers as suggested, you may need to place small wedges behind the ring for support. After the glue cures, mount the bowl on the lathe and finish shaping the ring.

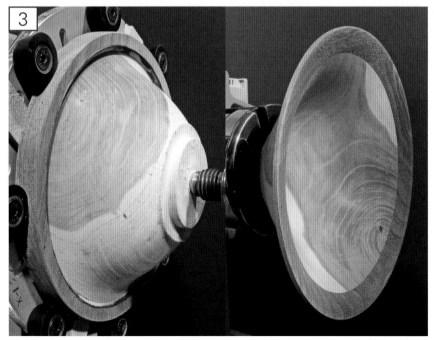

How to Add a Ring to the Rim of a Hollow Form

Suppose you are nearly finished hollowing a vessel and decide to add a ring of contrasting wood to the rim, either for esthetic considerations or to fix a problem with the existing rim.

Here's how to add a ring that sits proud of the vessel surface. If you want the ring to blend with the surface, cut the mating surfaces at an angle, as you would for a bowl with a rim that turns inward.

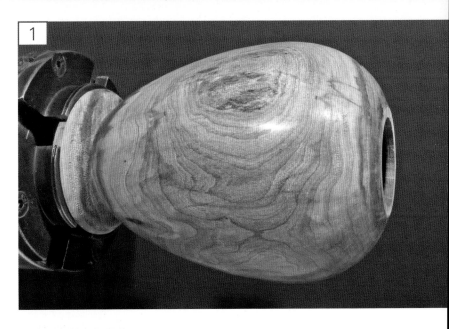

Step one. Prepare the rim of the vessel. Cut a flat surface around the rim and turn the opening to a cylinder with parallel sides. Leave the vessel mounted in the chuck and remove the assembly from the lathe.

Step two. Mount the blank for the ring on a screw chuck and turn it to a size slightly greater than the diameter of the flat on the vessel. Reduce the thickness of the disk if it is significantly greater than what you need for the rim. Mark the diameter of the opening in the vessel on the face of the disk. Mark a smaller diameter for the inner diameter of the finished ring. Cut a tenon on the ring so that it fits into the cylindrical opening of the vessel. Do test fits to sneak up on the right size for the tenon. Be sure that the tenon shoulder seats squarely against the flat surface on the vessel. Remove part of the waste wood from the interior of the rim, working around the center screw.

Step three. Remove the rim from the screw chuck and remount the vessel. Glue the ring and vessel together. Use the tailstock to apply clamping pressure. Once the glue has set, turn away the center section of the ring. This will allow you to judge the wall thickness of the ring, and the opening will serve as a reference as you shape the outer profile. Turn the inside surface of the ring and match its internal contour with that of the vessel. After a bit of sanding, the ring will be complete.

PROJECT: LIDDED BOX WITH OPTIMAL GRAIN MATCH

A box made of spalted maple (left) and one made of ash with a black walnut inset (right).

Many turners are pleased to make a lidded box that doesn't wobble and for which the lid fits reasonably well. Others take it to the next level and insist that the wood grain matches "perfectly" at the join between the lid and body. A method for optimizing the match is described here.

The key to getting a good match is to remove as little wood as possible between the lid and body. Typically, about ⅛" (3mm) or more is removed by the saw kerf or parting tool that separates the blank into two parts, one for the lid and one for the body. Another ⅜" (9.5mm) or so is lost to the tenon that secures the lid. This gives a net loss of about ½" (13mm), and the grain can wander significantly over this distance.

Consider this: if the tenon were made separately from another blank and then added to the body, we could significantly reduce the loss that arises from making the tenon as an integral part of the body. This is, in effect, what is described here. It is not hard to do.

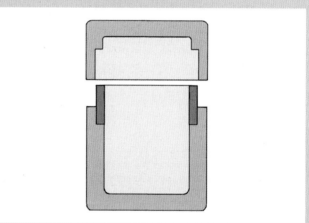

The cross section of the body and lid of a lidded box.

Credit: Paul Hedman of Moorehead, Minnesota.

Instructions for making a lidded box are published widely. Therefore, for brevity, only the steps involving the tenon are given here. We assume the body has been hollowed.

Step one. With the body mounted in a chuck, form the step where the tenon will be placed. Remove the body from the chuck.

Step two. To make the tenon, install a short spindle blank of a dense hardwood in the chuck. True it up. Use turning tools or a Forstner bit to hollow the end of the spindle to a depth of about 1" (25mm). Leave a wall thickness of at least ¼" (6mm).

Step three. Reduce the outside diameter of the tenon until it matches the step formed in the body of the box. Try to achieve an easy sliding fit.

Step four. Considering the dimensions of the step in the body and the amount you want the tenon to extend above the body, mark the blank where the cut should be made to remove the "tenon ring" from the blank. Make the cut.

Step five. Put the body back on the chuck. Glue the tenon ring into the body using ordinary wood glue or epoxy. After the glue cures, turn away the inside surface of the ring until it's flush with the inside surface of the body. The tenon is now finished and you can proceed with completing the rest of the box in the usual manner.

9 Ways to Make and Join Stackable Elements

Assembled pieces often consist of elements that vary widely in diameter, such as a skinny finial attached to a wide base, or an elevated footed vessel with a small-diameter stem attached to a much larger foot. Making a piece from several components not only reduces the amount of waste, it also allows you to orient the wood grain optimally. Thin stems require the grain to run lengthwise, but it is best to have side grain in a wide, flat

Elevated vessels The finials are made from elements joined together.

foot. Tenons and matching recesses make joining the elements a simple matter.

The following illustrations show several different types of stackable elements, each with a suggested chucking sequence shown in the drawings below each photo. Most of the blanks are side grain, cut from ¾" (19mm) flat stock. You can jam the blank against the jaws of a scroll chuck to true it up and turn a tenon on the tailstock side. If necessary, you can then reverse the blank to form a tenon on the opposite side.

In most cases, the jam chuck employed in the final step can be a simple flat surface turned on an endgrain blank held in a scroll chuck. To hold the piece against the jam chuck, the point of the live center is applied to the center of a recess or tenon. In either case, the mark left by the point does not show in the finished piece.

Stacked Hollow Forms

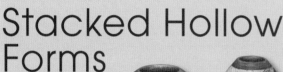

The parts of the stack. Three hollow forms, a base, and a small bowl.

These three stackable hollow forms were intended to be a serious composition in the vertical dimension. But the result was a whimsical piece unimagined at the outset.

The wood, spalted willow, was so punky that the jaws of the chuck simply crushed the tenon. Further, it was impossible to get a clean cut at the rim. I solved both problems by attaching rims and feet made of red cedar. The bowl (hat) is apple. The heights of the hollow forms are 5¼", 5½", and 4½" (133, 140, and 114mm). The diameters are 7", 5¾", and 4" (178, 146, and 102mm). The "stack" is 17" (432mm) tall.

Aha! I created a snowman.

Base for a pedestal, with recess

1. Turn tenons on each side of a disk.
2. Grip tenon A in a scroll chuck. Drill the hole for the recess in tenon B and shape the top of the piece as much as possible.
3. Reverse the piece, holding it by tenon B. Turn away tenon A and shape the bottom of the piece.
4. Jam chuck the piece, with a cone center to support it, and finish shaping the top of the piece.

Base for a pedestal, with recess

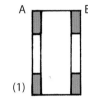 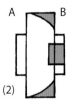 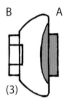 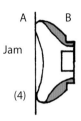

Base for a pedestal, with tenon

1. Turn a tenon (tenon B) on one side of a disk.
2. Grip the tenon in a scroll chuck. Form a second tenon, which will remain on the piece. At the base of this tenon, form another tenon greater in diameter (tenon A).
3. Reverse the piece, holding it by tenon A. Turn away tenon B and shape the bottom of the piece.
4. Jam chuck the piece and finish shaping the top.

Base for a pedestal, with tenon

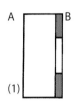 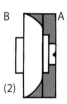  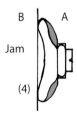

Base of a finial for a hollow form

1. Turn a tenon (tenon A) on one side of a disk.
2. Grip tenon A in a scroll chuck. Turn tenon B, keeping it larger than its finished diameter. Shape the inside of the flange.
3. Grip tenon B in a scroll chuck. Partially shape the top and drill the recess (or form a tenon).
4. Grip tenon A. Refine the flange that will extend into the opening of the vessel.
5. Jam chuck the piece to finish detailing the top.

Base for a finial that fits in the opening of a hollow form

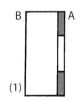    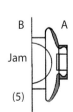

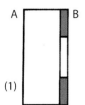
Element with a tenon and a recess

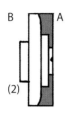
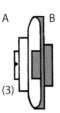
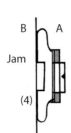

Element with a tenon and a recess

1. Turn a tenon (tenon B) on one side of a disk.

2. Grip the tenon in a scroll chuck. Form the tenon that will remain on the piece. At the base of this tenon, form another tenon greater in diameter (tenon A).

3. Reverse the piece, holding it by tenon A. Turn away tenon B, flatten the face, and drill the recess. Shape the bottom of the piece.

4. Jam chuck the piece to finish detailing the top.

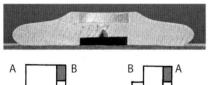
Element with two recesses

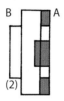
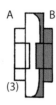
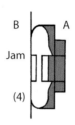

Element with two recesses

1. Turn a tenon (tenon B) on one side of a disk.

2. Grip tenon B in a scroll chuck. Turn tenon A and drill a deep recess into it.

3. Grip tenon A. Turn away tenon B and drill the second recess. Shape this side of the piece.

4. Reverse the piece and jam chuck it. Turn away tenon A and refine the shape of this side of the piece.

Stem-to-bowl transition piece for a vessel

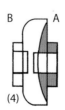
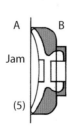

Stem-to-bowl transition piece for a vessel

1. Turn a tenon (tenon B) on one side of a disk.

2. Grip tenon B in a scroll chuck. Turn tenon A and drill a deep recess into it.

3. Grip tenon A. Drill a deep recess into tenon B and begin shaping that side of the piece.

4. Grip tenon B. Turn away tenon A and shape that side of the piece to match the profile of the base of the vessel.

5. Jam chuck the piece, turn away tenon B, and shape the profile where it will join the top of the stem.

Ring

1. Form a tenon (B) on one side of a disk.

2. Grip the tenon in a scroll chuck. Drill a hole in the disk that will form the opening. Drill slightly deeper than the finished ring thickness; leave ample material near the chuck.

3. Shape the outer surface of the ring.

4. Part off the ring, as indicated by the dashed lines in the drawing. If necessary, mount the ring on a single-ended mandrel to clean it up.

One-piece base for a vessel

1. Mount an endgrain blank between centers; form a tenon at each end. Mount the blank in a scroll chuck, with the top of the base at the tailstock end. Drill a deep recess.

2. Reverse the workpiece; grip tenon B in a scroll chuck. Use the tailstock for support. Remove waste wood from the center. Turn away tenon A; shape the base bottom.

3. Jam chuck the piece; remove the tenon and refine the top.

Knob for a lid

1. Mark the center on an endgrain blank and mount it in the scroll chuck. Turn it round, with a short tenon at one end.

2. Refine the shoulder around the tenon for a good fit with the lid. Shape body. Use the tailstock for support.

3. Reverse the turning; mount it in the collet chuck.

4. Using the tailstock to support the work, remove the waste at the knob top.

5. Move the tailstock and finish shaping the knob.

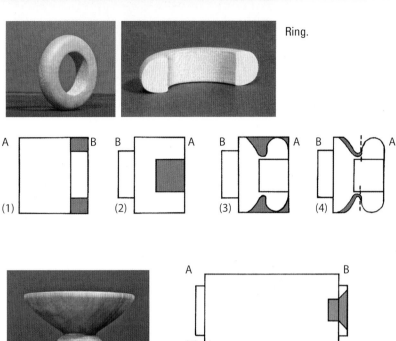

Ring.

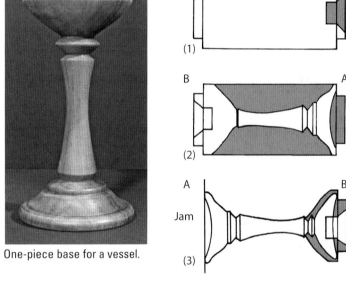

One-piece base for a vessel.

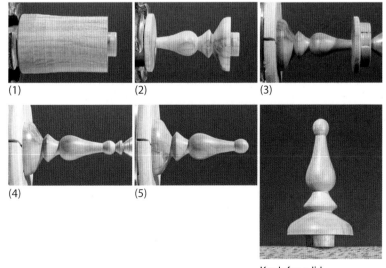

Knob for a lid.

Two Ways to Turn a Hollow Vessel

Turning a hollow vessel with a small opening isn't as difficult as it may seem. Here are two methods.

A vessel in two parts

Shape the outer profile of the vessel, then cut it into two parts. Hollow each part separately, then glue them back together. You can add a decorative groove, beads, or surface texture to hide the line where the two parts join.

Step one. Mount a blank between centers and turn the outer profile. Allow for the width of the parting cut as you shape the profile. Form a tenon at each end of the blank to fit a scroll chuck. Use a parting tool to cut part-way through, then finish with a hand saw. Mount the bottom section in a scroll chuck and hollow the interior. Flatten the rim to form a glue surface. Repeat this procedure for the top section.

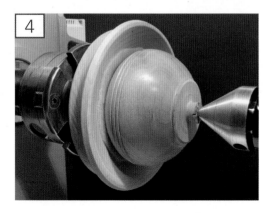

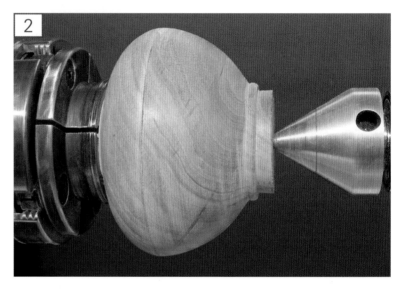

Step two. Apply wood glue to the rim of each part. Use a cone center on the tailstock to center the bottom section and maintain pressure while the glue sets.

Step three. Refine the profile. Grip the tenon at the bottom of the vessel and use the tailstock to support the work. Remove the tenon from the top. Turn or drill a small opening in the top center to check the wall thickness. Refine the area around the rim, which may include enlarging the opening and adjusting the wall thickness. If you want to add decorative elements at the rim and along the glue line, do them now.

Step four. Use a jam, doughnut, or vacuum chuck to hold the top while you finish the foot. If the top surface is flat, use a large-diameter jam chuck. If you use a vacuum chuck, make it large. I used a foam-padded jam chuck with a tenon at the center to fit into the opening. If you use normal jam-chucking, remove the nubbin after turning.

A vessel hollowed through the bottom

A bud vase, or weedpot, which has a long neck and a small opening at the rim, presents a challenge for hollowing the body. It is not always necessary to hollow the body, but removing some of the weight makes for a more elegant piece. The trick is to do the hollowing through an opening at the bottom, then plug this opening. If you make the body and plug from the same region of the blank, you can hide the fact that the opening ever existed.

The need for decorative work at the top and bottom of the piece complicates the chucking. The rim has to be detailed, and it is desirable to add decorative grooves to the bottom to hide the glue line around the plug. You can get vibration or chatter if you try to make a fairly tall piece supported only at the headstock end. Using a steady rest to stabilize the piece eliminates vibration and lets you make the piece as tall as your drilling and hollowing capabilities allow.

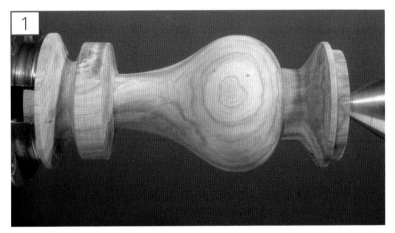

Step one. Mount a blank between centers and turn it to a cylinder. Form a tenon at each end. If you use a scroll chuck, be sure the center point at each end is marked. Mount the blank between a scroll chuck and a point center, with the bottom next to the tailstock. Rough out the profile. Allow room at the tailstock end to make the plug for the hole in the bottom. Leave the part of the piece that will have the largest diameter (close to the tailstock end) slightly oversize to provide a surface for the rollers of the steady rest. Leave a section near the headstock end almost full diameter to provide a second surface for the steady.

Weed Pots. These vases are hollowed from the bottom.

2

Step two. Reverse the piece and set up the steady rest. Use a scroll chuck to lightly grip the tenon at the bottom. Set the steady in place so that the rollers run on the large-diameter section near the rim. Bring up the tailstock point center to support the end of the piece. Tighten the chuck. Press the rollers against the piece and tighten the carriers. Back the tailstock away.

Step three. Drill a hole in the neck. Make it deep enough to extend into the body. Shape the rim tip, flaring the hole near the rim. Cut part of the tenon away so the rim stands proud of the end by about ³⁄₁₆" (5mm). Give the rim its final shape. Be sure that the distance between the tenon shoulder and the tip of the rim is less than the depth of your chuck jaws. Sand the interior by wrapping sandpaper around a dowel and inserting it. Sand the rim tip.

3

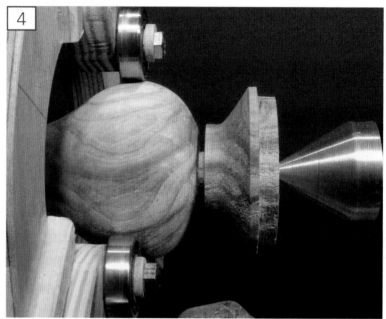

4

Step four. Reverse the piece and remove the end section. Grip the tenon at the rim, and bring up the tailstock point center for support while setting up the steady. Adjust the steady so the rollers run on the largest diameter. Mark the end of the piece so you can align the grain when you plug the opening. Use a parting tool and then a hand saw (with the lathe turned off) to remove the end section of the blank. Clean up the end of the piece.

Step five. Bore a hole and do the hollowing. Choose a bit with a diameter smaller than what the opening will be. Drill deep enough to join the hole through the neck. Enlarge the opening, but be careful not to make it larger than the diameter of the blank you removed in step four. Hollow the body. Remove weight from the bottom, but do not make the wall so thin that the finished piece feels top heavy. Form a slight taper on the inside wall of the opening so the plug will tighten as it is pressed into the hole. Remove the piece from the chuck.

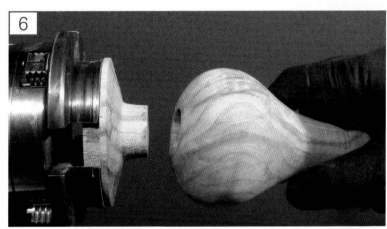

Step six. Put the end section you removed in step four back in the chuck. Shape the plug for the bottom, testing the fit often. Press the vessel onto the plug and rotate it by hand to make a burnish mark to indicate where material should be removed. The plug should extend into the opening an amount equal to the wall thickness around the opening.

Step seven. When the plug fits properly, align the grain and glue it in place. Use a cone center on the tailstock to maintain pressure while the glue sets. If you use a cone center made of aluminum, pad it with a thin layer of paper to prevent the aluminum from marking the piece.

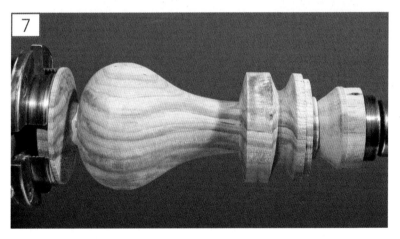

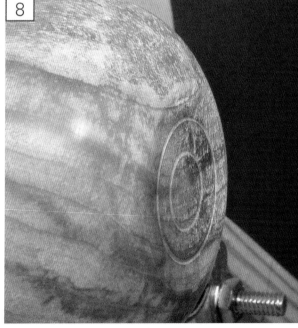

Step eight. Reverse the piece to finish the bottom, gripping the tenon at the rim. Set up the steady rest with the rollers against the body. Using tailstock support as long as possible, remove the tenon and waste wood from the bottom. Shape the bottom and make a shallow groove at the glue line. A second, smaller groove adds to the decorative effect. Sand the bottom and the adjacent portion of the body to completion.

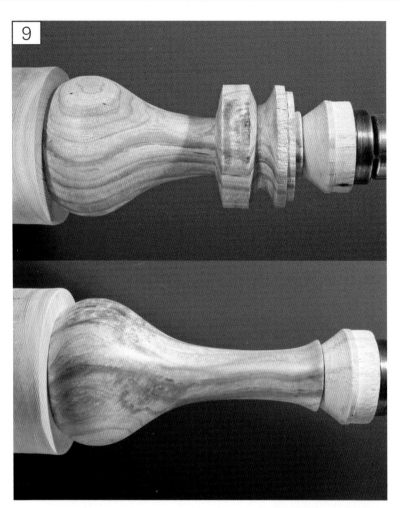

Step nine. Make a jam chuck that matches the contour of the bottom part. Use only thin padding, if any, so the piece will be held firmly and run true. Press the piece against the jam chuck, using a cone center inserted into the neck of the piece. Pad the cone center or use one made of wood to protect the workpiece. Complete the outer profile of the piece and sand it to completion.

Step ten. Blend the sanded regions. If you see a noticable difference between the regions sanded in steps eight and nine, make a single-ended mandrel to fit the neck opening and press the piece onto the mandrel. You can then blend the sanded regions.

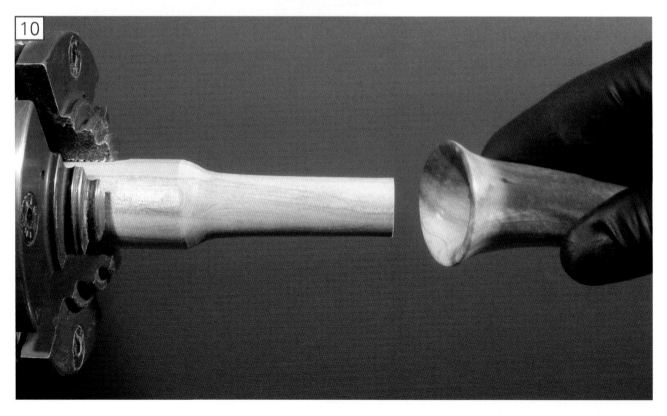

INDEX

Note: Page numbers in *italics* indicate projects